HAUNTED
POOLE

HAUNTED
POOLE

JULIE HARWOOD

The History Press

First published in 2007 by Tempus Publishing

Reprinted in 2011 by
The History Press
The Mill, Brimscombe Port,
Stroud, Gloucestershire, GL5 1RW
www.thehistorypress.co.uk

Reprinted 2012

British Library Cataloguing in Publication Data.
A catalogue record for this book is available from the British Library.

ISBN 978 0 7524 4503 8

Typesetting and origination by Tempus Publishing
Printed in Great Britain

CONTENTS

ACKNOWLEDGEMENTS

I would like to thank the following people for their help and contributions without whom this book would not have been possible: the writings and tour of Granny Cousins also known as Michelle O'Brien; David Austin, Parkstone; Catherine Drudge, Parkstone; Anita Habgood, Canford Heath; John and Shirley Hatton, Canford Heath; the family of Mr Alfred Russell; Poole Borough Council; Ann Smeaton, Hamworthy; Simon and Rachel Steadman, friends and fellow paranormal investigators; Shaun Spencer-Perkins, Poole Stadium general manager; Anna and the management of the Lord Nelson Pub; Heather Hogg (Heather V.) for allowing me to use some of her wonderful pictures of modern-day Poole; *The Bournemouth & Poole Daily Echo* – Newsquest Media Group; Jackie Spencer, Littledown in Bournemouth; Sheila and Marcus, Pinner; Ann Smeaton for her help with the story of Lake House.

Thanks to the many others that prefer to remain anonymous but who have helped me with this book, as well as my boyfriend Tony and my family and friends who have all listened patiently to me whittle on for years about 'ghosts!'.

All photographs unless stated are by Julie Harwood.

BIBLIOGRAPHY

Comotti, G., *Music in Greek and Roman Culture* Baltimore: John Hopkins, 1989

Cullingford Cecil N., *A History of Poole and Neighbourhood* Phillimore & Co., 1988

Ellis, Chris and Owens, Andy, *Haunted Dorset* SB Publications, 2004

Jones, Richard, *Haunted Inns of Britain & Ireland* New Holland Publishers UK, 2004

Joyce, Ray, *The Story of Poole on DVD*, December 2005

Knott, Oliver, Tales of Dorset Sherborne, 1975

Smeaton, Ann C., *A History of Hamworthy – Facts, Fables and Folk* 1ST Edition 2005

Wilnecker, Patricia M., *Ghostly Tales of Wessex,* 1995

The tiled 'welcome' to people arriving in Poole on the Bramble Bush Bay chain ferry.

INTRODUCTION

The town of Poole, with a population estimated at 141,000, lies on the south coast of the England in the county of Dorset. For many years it has been a popular destination with holidaymakers from home and abroad, with its fishing-town charm, wonderful countryside and close proximity to sister town Bournemouth. In the summer the town is crowded with tourists and locals flocking to the town and quay. Only the comings and goings of pleasure boats, cruisers and yachts from the quayside rival the hustle and bustle of the town. Twinned with Cherbourg, Poole has also enjoyed a good relationship with its French neighbours for over twenty years.

Poole boasts the second largest natural harbour in the world and has been a functioning port for hundreds of years. Now, however, the shallow waters stop the harbour from welcoming the larger cargo ships. Brownsea Island, where the Scouting Movement began in 1907, has been a nature reserve since 1964 and along with the harbour is an ecological area, supporting varied habitats.

Poole has an interesting and colourful history and has been inhabited for over 2,000 years. The most interesting archaeological find to date is the Poole log boat (made from one oak tree) dating back to 295BC.

When the Romans invaded Britain in the first century, Poole was a popular landing site; its name derived from the old English word 'Pol' (a name given to people that lived by a small area of water).

When the Romans retreated, the town's trade suffered although small communities stayed in the area. William Longspee presented Poole with its first charter in 1248 but it was not until the Norman Conquest that Poole's trade began to grow again with the export of wool to Spain. In 1405 most of the town was set alight when the Spanish retaliated after being attacked by local pirates but despite this, it was rebuilt and continued to thrive. Salt was now the largest commodity and the warehouses storing the product dominated the quayside by the seventeenth century. By the nineteenth century most inhabitants of Poole were employed in the harbour in one capacity or another and workers moved into the area to take advantage of its job opportunities and the high standard of living. Subsequently the villages around Poole grew until they merged, and Poole's sister town, Bournemouth, was born.

A view over Poole Harbour.

Today Poole retains clues to its industrial and maritime heritage. I have lived in the town for five years and cannot imagine living anywhere else. Poole residents complain that every summer they are invaded by tourists, yet they whinge with pride – pride that so many people want to visit their hometown.

I have always been interested in the paranormal and things that 'go bump in the night' and when I moved to Poole I felt I was a child being shown a sweet shop for the first time! Before long, I formed a paranormal investigation team, Southern Paranormal UK and after visiting some of the places in our region, the team were left with no doubt that England's south coast has some of the best haunting tales in the country, with history to back them up. Every local has a tale to tell, whether it is about a phantom pirate or a white lady. Some of these are stories handed down through the generations in a family, others are first-hand encounters and accounts of strange experiences. Many are well-known haunting stories while others have stayed secret for many years and are known to only a few. Some are tales that have never been told before. Some believe distressed spirits still wander the town with unfinished business while others believe it is a mere paranormal recording of times gone by replaying again and again. Only a few people have been happy to confirm or deny knowledge of the stories for me; it still seems that paranormal is a bit of a taboo subject people don't like to talk about but almost everyone, whether they believe or not, has an opinion, even if it is just a view that is shared in private among friends. I have put pen to paper to record the accounts that have been related to me or that I have heard about, but I cannot personally vouch for the truth behind the stories and many of the reports have remained unconfirmed. However, the purpose of the book is not to prove or disprove the paranormal or the existence of ghosts. Instead it is to disclose a little local history with each story and tell the fascinating tales of haunted Poole and let you, the reader, decide for yourself.

CHAPTER ONE

THE QUAY AND
OLD TOWN

The Phantom Toll Collector

The existing Poole lifting bridge which connects Poole old town and Hamworthy built in 1927 was preceded by two other bridges in an attempt to join the two areas that are separated by a busy shipping channel. The bridge lifts up to seven times a day to allow larger vessels through and approximately 20,000 cars cross it daily. The bridge today is a public highway which means anyone is free to cross although before 1927 it was privately owned and tolls for crossing were payable to the owner. Local MP William Ponsonby was responsible for the first bridge over the channel in 1834. This wooden bridge was steep, making it almost impossible for horses to cross and as they were the main form of transport at the time this posed a huge problem. In 1885 it was replaced by an iron structure which was much easier to cross but with high tolls not everyone could afford the charge and some people still had no choice but to use the longer route round the perimeter of the town. The high tolls of this bridge bear some relation to the haunting that is supposed to surround it. Cars have been known to stop at the beginning of the bridge at night when the dark figure of a man steps into the road in front of them. Drivers often screech to a halt, not seeing him until the last minute and are scared they will hit him. He apparently looks at the car before shaking what looks to be an old tin, and then disappears as quickly as he appeared. Could this be the infamous 'Poole Bridge Collector', an uncompromising and unfriendly man employed by the landowners to collect the tolls due to them?

The Jumper

On Poole Quay between the lifting bridge and Yeatmans Mill stands what is considered to be the biggest eyesore in Poole. Built in the mid-twentieth century this mass of concrete is now derelict and in a poor state and has been empty since 1987. Before that it served as a grain silo but since the decline in local milling the firm abandoned the premises. A local company

Will you meet the phantom toll collector when crossing the bridge?

now owns the site with plans for major developments of quayside apartments, however due to various planning and constructive issues it still stands empty behind a wire fence, a shell of its former self. In its heyday it would have been alive with staff employed in many roles on the site. Prior to there being a grain silo there, there was a similar mill standing only yards away. Many similar buildings stood on the quay taking direct deliveries of grain from shipments arriving there. The current building's tragic end ties in with the sad story of a suicidal man seen at the site.

The building is five-stories high and the man in question has been sighted on the roof of the structure, on the right-hand side on a walkway. Dressed all in white, he peers over the railings, looking down at the quay below. Many people have seen him and some have been known to call out to him. The reports of sightings differ very little – all who see him say he leans over the railings as if looking for something. He then sits on the railings and swings his legs over, still looking down at the ground below. At this point some people have been known to call the local

The derelict mill – still home to a very sad spirit.

This tiny lane echoes its past visitors.

police in horror thinking he may jump. He certainly has death on his mind, as seconds after sitting on the railings, he throws himself off. Horrifyingly he disappears as soon as he jumps, leaving some people gasping with a mixture of shock and disbelief. So what keeps him here, possibly reliving the way he died? Strangely there are no known reports of a suicide taking place at this site. For hundreds of years documents were sketchy and the further back in time they were written the less chance there is of finding reliable or complete records. There is no timescale on the sighting so it is not known what era he lived. What does tie him to the silo site is the fact he appears to use the railings that can clearly be seen at the top of the building. Previous buildings on the site had sloped roofs and certainly did not have the metal railings that the current building has. So is this an unknown death? Maybe this tormented spirit returns to the site because his sad demise was not recorded or recognised in any way. We may never know, but one thing is for sure, according to the people I have spoken to, the jumper is one of the most commonly seen spirits in the town. Despite being one of the most witnessed sightings it is mentioned infrequently probably ,because of the trauma suffered by the onlooker. Ironically it is also one of the most unknown hauntings in Poole.

St Clements Lane

If you walk down a little alleyway known as St Clements Lane, close to the quayside, you can visit some of the oldest parts of Poole and you will eventually reach parts of the old town walls. It is said that it is down this little alley in 1248 that William Longspee the 2nd Lord of the Manor of Canford, met to arrange the sale of the little fishing town of La Pole to guildsmen. This allowed them some freedom from the feudal rights of the manor and to run the town as they wished by giving the people of La Pole or Poole the right to elect six men to form a borough council. This was a significant date in the history of Poole and it enabled Longspee to raise funds for his seventh crusade. The charter is now safely stored in the town's waterfront museum as a reminder of the price of the town's freedom. Though this little inconspicuous alley lies nearly out of view, on some nights it is said you can still hear Longspee himself talking to the men he was meeting, trying to raise the best sums he could for his crusade before sealing the deal. The rights bestowed by Longspee are still upheld to this day and every May the annual Mayor-Making Ceremony is held in Poole. The mayor, deputy mayor and sheriff are elected and given their duties for the time they are in office. The mayor also has additional duties as mayor of the staple, clerk of the market and admiral of the port of Poole. On this day in May, it is said that if you look very carefully during the Mayor's Parade you can see the face of William Longspee in the crowd watching over primarily what he created.

Yeatman's Mill

Built in the eighteenth century, Yeatman's Mill has been the home of the Yeatman family, for over 100 years. Anthony and Wendy Yeatman, the current owners, converted the building in 1976 but retained as much of its 'old world' charm and original features as possible. It is situated on Poole Quay between the lifting bridge and the Customs House and now accommodates La Lupa Italian restaurant and luxurious holiday apartments. Its tall, narrow frontage, like many buildings on the quay is deceptive – its depth indicates that it probably employed many local people. During the renovation of the building old smugglers' passages were discovered and although they are now blocked up it appears its former users are still resident, according to one local who was contracted to do work for the family in the 1980s. A large, strong man, he refused to ever step foot in the place again when he was tapped on the shoulder whilst working only to find there was no one else in the room with him. Chilled to the bone by the sudden coldness in the area he went into a coughing fit due to the sudden overwhelming smell of tobacco and alcohol. Petrified he finished the job, collected his tools and left as soon as he could.

The old harbour office. (Heather V.)

The Old Harbour Office

The old Harbour Office, originally built in 1727, stands opposite the Customs House on the old quay and was built as a reading room for the local merchants. This is the oldest part of Poole Quay and is shown on older maps of the area as the 'Great Quay'. In 1822 the original harbour office building was knocked down and a newer structure replaced it. The building was similar to a library containing reading matter specific to merchants such as maps and trade accounts; it also provided them with a meeting place. This is where the ghost of a Poole mayor is supposed to be still roaming. Benjamin Skutt who was Mayor of Poole in 1717, 1727 and 1742 has been sighted here wearing his mayoral regalia including a wig. A mayor is always thought to be seen in a town hall but during this period most would have been merchants or born into wealthy merchant families as Skutt was. His plaque/picture hangs on the side wall of the Harbour Office, which now houses the local headquarters for HM Coastguard.

The King Charles Inn, 1905.

Romeo and Juliet

Just off the quay at the beginning of Thames Street is the King Charles Inn. Originally this building was called the New Inn but was renamed when King Charles X of France (having recently abdicated) docked at Poole Quay in 1830. After leaving Poole, King Charles set sail to Lulworth Castle further up the Purbeck coast. This impressive pub was extended in 1788 when the massive town cellars were cut through creating Thames Street. The main section of the inn was built in the Tudor period and the oriel windows and black-and-white timber-framed walls bear justice to its history. Large black doors hide a storeroom from the street and the secrets of what may have been kept in the room over the years. Today it is hired to Poole's regular visitor, the French onion seller. Stepping inside the inn the visitor is transported back in time as the building retains most of its original features such as beautiful wooden wall panelling, old beams and a stunning fireplace. The inn is said to be haunted and most people presume the ghost is King Charles X of France, however this does not appear to be the case. There are no conclusive reports that he ever visited the inn, only that it was named in his honour. The actual tale of the resident ghosts is a much sadder one. There have been many experiences of suspected

The King Charles Inn, 2007.

paranormal activity in the pub. These include bottles and glasses smashing for no apparent reason, heavy footsteps heard in the middle of the night, items disappearing for no reason and owner's pets refusing to even enter certain parts of the pub including many of the rooms upstairs. Visitors and residents, especially women, also notice a feeling of sadness and desperation hanging in the air. The ghosts that are said to haunt the pub are a pretty but sad young lady, and a sailor.

In the eighteenth century the pub's landlady fell deeply in love with a local sailor and they pledged their devotion to each other. He had to set sail on a long journey so the pair promised to stay true to each other until his return when they would get married. Months later when the sailor was due to return, a huge storm hit the seas and when he did not arrive back the landlady feared he had been killed at sea. In desperation she took a thick rope and hung herself from one of the upstairs beams. Only a matter of days later, exhausted from his treacherous journey, the sailor returned to the inn to be reunited with his sweetheart. When he arrived at the inn he found it unusually locked and had to break in. He found his love still hanging in the upstairs room. Distraught beyond all belief the heartbroken young sailor is said to have pulled her down from the rope and then in a fit of despair and grief, with a knife, took his own life.

This is truly Poole's own Romeo and Juliet story and it is said the pair remain in the building trying to reunite with each other, the lady repentant because of the way she pointlessly ended her own life and the sailor reliving the night he found his true love hanging. If you visit the inn it is said that you are likely in one way or another to experience the tortured souls of the couple. Apparently most people notice cold spots, feel someone sitting next to them or smell the sweet fragrance of lavender water when the lady is near. When the sailor is around, there is said to be an overwhelming aroma of the sea and the feeling of anger.

Smuggling Spooks

Sarum Street runs off of Thames Street and lies directly behind the old town cellars, now know as the Waterfront Museum and History Centre. A partly cobbled street still remains and

The cutting of the town walls created Thames Street.

This is where the spirits of smugglers run as they rush past pedestrians on Sarum Street.

it is believed that on some nights if you walk around here you will feel a cold breeze and the sensation of many people pushing past you as if in a hurry to get somewhere. They are thought to be a gang of local pirates, the area having been a quick escape from their landing point on the quay. It is reported that you may also be able to smell burning and this is believed to be a 'place memory' of when the town's cellars that originally stood there completely encircling the old town, were burnt to the ground in 1405. Even though this is one of the main connecting roads to the old town some locals refuse to walk down it at night in fear they may run into Poole's old crooks!

Anything to Declare?

The most recognisable building on Poole Quay is without a doubt the Georgian Customs House. The present building was erected in 1814 although there has been a Custom & Excise House on this site since 1756. The original building was destroyed by fire in 1813 and subsequently another one had to be built hurriedly as trade into the port at this time was thriving. By the 1960s this great Grade II Listed landmark had fallen into disrepair and lay derelict until a local restaurateur purchased it in 1991, turning it into a stylish and popular *a la carte* restaurant. Luckily the new owners renovated the building sympathetically and by the mid-1990s it was restored to its former glory, including the front of the building, where a town beam has been placed (town beams were used to weigh goods for customs duty). Its colourful past bring tourists flocking to admire its grandeur.

An incident at the Customs House has gone down in British smuggling history. In 1747 the infamous Jack Diamond was captured here and his smuggled tea stored at the Customs House. Angry that their cargo had been seized, the rest of Jack's men (who were in fact his brothers) enlisted the help of the Hawkhurst gang from Kent. Armed, they stormed Poole one night and battered down the door of the Customs House taking back all the tea and freeing Jack. It was a bloody battle between smugglers and guards but the smugglers got away with as much of the precious commodity as they could. It is believed there could have been up to sixty in the gang that night but only fourteen men were subsequently captured and hung for their crimes. It is believed that a member named Carter was one of the gang who informed authorities of the whereabouts and identities of the smugglers after the raid and he was taken by Jack and the remaining gang to a local well where he was stoned and drowned for his betrayal.

Local legend suggests that the dark figure of a man often seen on the top floor of the Customs House is that of Carter returning to the scene of the crime looking to avenge his murder. Staff at the Customs House have often sensed a feeling of being watched.

However, another spirit also said to roam the building and area outside is that of a Captain Johnson, the man responsible for seizing the contraband that fateful year. It is believed he still patrols the quay keeping a lookout for suspicious cargo and activity. Johnson was a local man who took such pride in his job that he still carries it out to this day. A man in a dark coat and wide-brimmed hat has been seen by a number of people, seemingly floating by the quayside. When approached the figure simply turns and disappears.

Poole Poltergeist

The Quay pub now owned by J.D. Wetherspoon stands towards the easterly end of the quay. It is a pub popular with visitors and is rarely less than half full. It was originally a warehouse used for imported goods, and although it has been completely transformed inside, people working in the pub sense that something from the past is lingering and trying to attract their attention. One night as four of the staff were clearing up they heard a glass smash at the rear of the pub, making them all jump. They went to investigate and found no one there; even stranger was that there were no pieces of glass to be found! The staff felt on edge, especially the four that were working there the night of the incident as they had already felt and sensed

The scene of the 1747 Customs House robbery.

odd sensations around the building. Much of the activity seemed to centre on the back of the pub and several staff experienced immense fear, and refused to go into the area. On many occasions workers have felt that someone or something was stopping them from entering the back of the pub. It was around this time that some staff also experienced sensations of being poked and prodded.

One day an employee was prodded quite hard and painfully in the ribs. She swung round ready to confront the person believing that one of the other members of staff was playing about, only to find no one anywhere near her. Early one morning the manager was called out to the premises as the motion-sensing alarms had been triggered. When he arrived some of them were being triggered in series, one after the other, and the only way this could happen was if someone was walking around the bar.

Another morning, two employees started work early. Knowing they were the only people in the building, they were surprised when they could hear a sound which they described as similar to a metal spoon being stirred in a china cup. When they went to investigate the area from which the sound was coming from everything was silent.

There are also stories of objects going missing and odd breathing noises being heard but no one has ever seen anything. Is someone trying to get the staff's attention or is this poltergeist activity? Staff have made considerable efforts to trace the history of the building to discover clues as to why they were experiencing the strange phenomena but have not found anything that could give them any details. All they know is that the warehouse, like other warehouses on the quay, had been a hive of activity and maybe it is someone from this era that still haunts the pub.

The Old Seadog

On the quay you will find the Old Seaman's Mission occupied today by a local restaurateur but one of its older residents still remains. On the second floor of the building, reports are made of people hearing heavy footsteps and a gruff coughing sound, and the apparition of an old man with a long grey beard and cloth cap has been seen sitting in a chair in the corner. The first floor of the building used to be a missionary chapel providing a base for Christian missionary work in the town. It would also have provided a place for seamen to live while they worked on the quay. Is the old seadog seen there a former mission resident unwilling to move on? Is there a reason he haunts just the floor that occupied the chapel? There is nothing reported that is menacing about this old man so people seem happy to just share their space with him.

The Old Seaman's Mission, now the Oriel Restaurant on the quay.

Even though the channel has become shallower over the years some large boats are still able to dock at the quay.

The Lord Nelson

The Lord Nelson is popular with locals including the motorcycling community of Dorset who meet regularly on the quay. The pub was built in 1764 by Stephen Adey and was originally called the Blue Boar. In 1810 the landlord renamed it in memory of Lord Nelson who had been killed in battle several years earlier. The pub has entertained a few famous guests over the years, one of these being the well-known artist Augustus Edwin John. The Welshman loved Poole and in the 1920s resided here and frequented the pub often. John was leader of the New English Art Club and while he lived in Poole in 1921 was made a member of the Royal Academy. Is it John's ghost or that of the building's original owner Stephen Adey who haunts the pub? What is certain are the footsteps heard on the stairs leading up from the main area of the pub when there is no one climbing them or anywhere nearby. The sounds stop as soon as they start and are only heard very occasionally.

The Lord Nelson – still as popular a place to drink as it was when it was built in 1764.

The Fish Shambles

Trading of fresh fish in Poole has always been excellent and in the seventeenth century the town established the fish shambles (otherwise know as a fish market) on the end of the quay. Even though local fish had been sold in the town market prior to this, it was the first market dedicated to the fisherman's catch. It provided an area for locals to sell their fish at competitive prices which could not be considered fresher being sold only 20ft away from the fishing boat from which it was caught. Unfortunately today, even though the name Fish Shambles remains, the area where the market took place is very different. It now houses kiosks selling fast food and drinks to tourists for half of the year but when trade is slow they close up and the area looks quite barren and empty. The only way to tell it was once a market is a plaque marking the start of the Cockle Trail, a historical walk through Poole charting the town's history which has been embedded in the floor of the shambles. If you visit the shambles at night though, you might get

Busy in the day but at night fisherman Pete's moans can still be heard at the old Fish Shambles.

more than you bargained for. After all the pubs' visitors have gone and the lights of the town have dimmed you may just meet fisherman Pete in need of some help. In the late 1780s during a busy market, a local fisherman stumbled into the crowd clutching his arm and shouting wildly for help. People just watched as the seemingly crazed man ranted and raved, when he dropped to the ground revealing a horrendous injury to his arm. The story says that while he was out fishing alone in his small boat one of the sail ropes became wrapped round his arm slicing it nearly to the bone. He managed to untangle himself enough to sail the boat slowly back to the quay but was bleeding heavily and by the time he reached the shore he was near to death. All he could do was stumble among the watching crowd. Unfortunately any attempts to save the man were in vain as he died where he fell. His unfortunate death is testament to this day of the dangers of lone sailing. It appears, however, that the ghost of the fisherman is not at rest. A misty figure of a man without an arm can be seen around the shambles and his screams and moans can still be heard as he seeks the help that he never received the day he died.

The lifeboat station where James Hughes served.

Hero James

Being one of the most visited shorelines in the country the presence of a lifeboat station in Poole has always been important. Before 1882 the boathouse was situated on Sandbanks. Early in 1882 a new station was built at the fisherman's dock, an area at the far eastern point of Poole Quay. The station still stands today and looks no different to the day it closed its doors for the final time in 1974. The building now houses a museum displaying the history and heritage of lifeboats and the centre welcomes many visitors each day. The new RNLI station now serves the shoreline and provides an essential rescue service. In 1939 the station on the quay received its very first motor lifeboat *Thomas Kirk Wright* and this was to become one of the nineteen lifeboats used in the evacuation of troops from Dunkirk in 1940. The men serving the lifeboat station over the years often risked their own lives to rescue others and even in the roughest of seas showed no fear in putting themselves in the line of danger and at the hands of 'mother nature'. Constant training was required for every level of rescue and this is something all crews had to do. These men put themselves in danger in every rescue carried out and it is ironic that an experienced member of the crew was killed during a training exercise.

James Hughes had taken part in many rescues but on the day he met his tragic end it was not even the sea that took his life. On 9 October 1884 he was crushed to death when he fell in front of the wheels of the carriage that pulled the lifeboat in and out of the water. He was getting out of the lifeboat after an exercise in the harbour with his crewmates, when he lost his footing, slipped and fell. Every effort was made to save him but James was just too badly injured by the crushing wheels. It was a tragic accident and one that the lifeboat community of Poole still remember to this day. Crew have been lost in action before but never has someone been lost on land whilst not in service. The lifeboat committee members donated £50 (considered a large sum in the late 1800s) to his family after his tragic death. James Hughes left behind a wife and small children and the station wanted to help support them as much as they could. His fellow crew sadly missed him.

To this day some people believe that James still wanders the fisherman's docks where the accident that took his life occurred. A black misty figure is seen on the slipway in front of the station and along the adjacent bit of the quay, undoubtedly where the accident took place and then where he eventually passed away. People have been know to have the overwhelming feeling of sadness and despair right in front of the boathouse and also some have been known to experience a crushing sensation around their middle of their body when standing at the water's edge. A man's voice has also been reported to have been heard calling 'I cannot go, I need to' but no one can make out exactly word for word what he says after this. Could these be James's last words to his crew that were trying to save his life? Is he frustrated that perhaps he did not have time to tell the men exactly what he wanted to?

One lady from Middlesex got more than she bargained for when she visited the Thistle Hotel. After dinner one night she and her partner decided to take a walk along the quay towards the town. Fascinated by history, her partner decided to have a look at the old lifeboat station and they wandered slowly over to it from the hotel. It was a clear night and the couple remembered that they could see the stars and there was little breeze as all the boat masts were uncharacteristically still and silent. As they wandered around the outside of the boathouse the lady felt quite nervous and also felt an icy chill in the air that she had not felt earlier. She put on the cardigan that she had been carrying and continued. As the couple walked back, the lady could see a mist had fallen over the water. The couple thought this strange as it was such a clear night but as they walked towards the water's edge the mist disappeared. Both remember looking at each other with a degree of bemusement at what they had just seen and it was at that moment that the lady swung round to look behind her. We all know that feeling of knowing someone is behind us even though we can not see or hear them and so she was surprised to find there was no one there and her partner was in front of her looking out towards Brownsea Island. It was he who turned around to face her and said 'I am James'. She stared at him wondering what he was talking about, as his name was not James or anything similar sounding but then she realised that the person at whom she was looking did not have the face of her partner. This man's face was a lot younger and slimmer and she noticed immediately he had sad eyes. He then shook his head in disbelief and said he just felt as though he had to say what he just said. His face returned to normal and the couple hesitantly laughed the episode off and decided to wander back to the hotel abandoning the rest of their walk that evening. The woman did not relate the apparent

The area of the quay where the spirit of James Hughes can still be felt.

face-change to her husband until later that night when neither could sleep and he surprised her by saying he felt that in that split second it was not him stood there and that he felt like someone else. So was this James trying to communicate through the man? The intriguing thing is the couple who told me this story had no interest in the paranormal beforehand and knew nothing of the history of the station. To say they were a little surprised when I told them about the tragic and untimely death of James is an understatement but the couple hope to return to Poole in the future and visit the old lifeboat station.

Anniversary D-Day Haunting

On the quay there is a plaque recording the part Poole played in operation Overlord, which was the code name for the allied invasion of Northwest Europe in 1944, during the Second World War. Poole was the third largest embarkation point for American troops leaving for Normandy on the north French coast. Poole played a large part in the preparations for the invasion including the housing of elite training bases, practice areas for troops and shipbuilding facilities where many of the landing craft were prepared for the invasion. Although Poole was prepared for war, the town was thought to be a prime bombing target and during the war years it became heavily fortified. Despite being such a prominent location during the operation, the area escaped major bombing with only three bombing raids hitting the town. The first bomb

The quay from Hamworthy, 1978. (Painted by Norah Rosewarne, a local artist)

that fell on Poole was in the Upper Parkstone area and the damage was recorded on film by a Mr Shepherd, a local man who owned one of the shops that was hit. The invasion of north-west Europe was without doubt a success and helped bring about the war's end, however many lives were lost in the process. The US army alone is estimated to have lost over 6,600 men on D-Day. It is said that on 6 June each year since the launch of the D-Day invasions in 1944, you can hear the US troops on the quay marching in preparation of their departure.

Ghostly Galleons

By the early fifteenth century there was a lot of unease in Europe especially between England, France and Spain and this led to many attacks on ports on the south coast. The man that led the British raiders was a man called Harry Paye. He lived in Hill Street in Poole and was a privateer and a commander of the Cinque Ports Fleet for the Admiral. He also earned the reputation of Poole's most well-known pirate and carried out raids on Normandy to the Bay of Biscay, which in turn led to further uprisings against the English in France and Spain. Harry Paye still features prominently in the Spanish historical accounts as a notorious pirate who ravaged the coasts of Poole, an unfortified port on the south coast and an easy target. The Spanish also believed it was

If Poole town is ever threatened you may see Harry Paye's ghostly galleon, the Mary, *protecting the harbour.*

where they were most likely to find Paye and in retaliation Spanish fleets were sent to attack Poole in 1405. The brave men of Poole fought as hard as they could to drive back their attackers but they were seriously outnumbered and after a fierce battle the town was set alight. The raiders, still not happy, went in search of Harry Paye. Paye, having heard of the attack, had fled causing the anger amongst the raiders who then sought out his brother and killed him.

When Paye returned to the town and learned of his brother's demise at the hands of the raiders he swore he would avenge them. Two years later Paye sailed to France with a fleet of just fifteen ships and captured over 100 French vessels which were bursting with cargos of iron, salt, lead and wine which he brought back to thank the men of Poole for defending the town as well as they could. It is said that the locals were drunk for a month after Paye arrived home with the cargo! Local legend believes that when Poole town is threatened in any way, Harry Paye's ghostly galleon the *Mary* guards the entrance from attack. Locals thank Harry for protecting them by holding an annual 'Harry Paye Day', usually in June, which is dedicated to the exploits of Great 'Arry Paye!'

The Whipped Woman

The chambers of the Guildhall will have seen much drama in the town unfold over the last couple of centuries. Punishments for crime were severe and often humiliating such as public whippings. Poole Quay for many years had what was known as a public whipping post. The sentenced men and women were taken down to the quay and amidst crowds of people were violently whipped. While many would have survived, a few in poorer health or weaker in spirit would have died at the hands of the whip or as a result of their wounds. This obviously depended on how many strikes of the whip they had been sentenced to. More severe whippings would have lasted sometimes as long as twenty minutes and this would have been for petty crimes that in present times would seem very minor, if criminal at all.

One woman who has been seen and sensed on Poole Quay could very well have been a victim of this harsh treatment. She is what is called an 'anniversary haunting' and only appears in the month of August. Could this be the month she suffered at the hand of the town whip? She is seen wearing a long green skirt and a cream blouse. On her back, blood can be seen seeping through her blouse from the inflicted wounds. No one knows who she is but she cannot be comforted and sobs as she stumbles along the quay before eerily disappearing into the night.

The Fishermen's Church

Nestled in the old town, on Thames Street is the parish church of St James. There has been a place of worship on this site for over 800 years but the Georgian church that stands there today was built in 1821. Effigies in the church can be dated as far back as the fourteenth century. Originally on this site there would have been an old wooden chapel serving the small population but as the town grew the church needed to expand to cater for its parishioners and by the sixteenth century a stone building had replaced the old wooden chapel. Local lore says that during the reign of King Edward VI, the Duke of Somerset demanded that eight of the church bells were sold and their profits put towards the town's fortification. Sadly the bells were sold but never

St James, the fisherman's church with its unusual fish-shaped weathervane.

made it to their new home as they were lost at sea on their way to Holland. Legend says that if you ever hear eight bells ring then Poole will be attacked. The church has long been with fishermen in the town and has become known over past centuries as the fishermen's church. It also boasts an unusual fish-shaped weathervane to seal its association. Local fisherman and their families would have made up a large part of its congregation in the sixteenth and seventeenth centuries and together they would have come to the church to pray for a good catch or the safe return of their boat and crew. When boats were lost at sea, families would lay wreaths outside the church in memory of their lost ones and in the hope that they still may return. In bad weather it is said that these spectral wreaths can be seen around the church in memory of the hundreds of fishermen that over the years have never returned home.

St James' Precinct

This area is the heart of Poole. In medieval times character buildings lined the area, as Poole became one of the most important and influential ports on the south coast. In 1497 a discovery was made that would change Poole and the lives of its inhabitants forever. John Cabot discovered Newfoundland whilst trying to find a western route to Asia. Having been granted permission by King Henry VII 'to search for unknown lands and bring back merchandise to Bristol', Cabot discovered one of the largest fishing grounds in the world. It is said that the seas were so full of cod that ships were unable to make passage safely. This news excited some of the more brave Poole mariners and by 1528 large quantities of salt used for fish salting were being imported into the town. From the late seventeenth century, when Newfoundland was recognised as British territory, the demand for fish meant that the town had an unforeseen period of prosperity. Few of the medieval buildings still stand today as the fine Georgian mansions built by the wealthy Newfoundland merchants took over the area in the eighteenth century. The merchants formed alliances, elite groups that became known as the 'Merchant Princes'. In 1802 records show that the merchants' prosperity was at its peak with the fleet in Poole having grown to over 360 ships.

In Thames Street stands Poole House. Built in the eighteenth century, it is apparently haunted by one of its previous owners, wealthy merchant Robert Slade. Slade was a well-known character in the community but his demise came about with many others when Napoleon was defeated in 1814. Through the Napoleonic Wars trade had flourished as countries such as Spain relied on Poole for their supplies of salt fish. The end of the war meant French and Americans could now fish the waters around Newfoundland and they could also serve the needs of other countries. In the years following, many of the Poole merchants had ceased trading and some were facing financial ruin. Robert Slade was no different and although he became Poole's mayor in 1835, his wealth was declining. He did not die a poor man but was a shadow of his former self. Could this be the reason he still haunts Poole House? The building itself has been changed and extended in many ways yet has retained its flamboyant façade and period splendour and so maybe this is what keeps the lonely merchant here, wandering around the house he called home in his happier days.

Church Street in Poole old town.

Spine-Chilling Double Murder

Scaplen's Court stands on the High Street and today is a museum and education centre. It is a magnificent example of a medieval domestic building and even though it has seen many changes over the years it still retains many of the original features from the fifteenth century. During the Civil War it was known as the George Inn and was used to house troops. In the old fireplaces dates and initials from that period are scratched into the stone. In the eighteenth century it was converted into a courtyard inn where prosperous merchants and tradesmen would have stayed. One such tradesman was John Scaplen. It is not known exactly when Scaplen acquired the building but it was used in a marriage settlement for his granddaughter in 1784 so it may be assumed to have been in his family for some time at this point. In the early 1900s many families lived in the building, however in 1920 a vicious storm ripped off the roof. Families inside grabbed what belongings they could and fled for cover elsewhere. By 1928 the building had begun to fall into disrepair. The Society of Poole Men raised £430 and restored the building, allowing it to be open to the public by 1929. Despite the restful and tranquil appearance of the house today, in the late 1500s it was the scene of a bloody double murder.

The murderer, a John Berryman and one of his victims Agnes Beard, apparently haunt the house and grounds of Scaplens Court and it is said if you are unlucky enough you are still able to hear the spine-chilling screams of his victims. Agnes was the servant of Alice Green, a rich widow who lived in the court, and on a fateful night in 1598 Berryman, who was the son-in-law of Green, came into the house with the intent to murder and steal from his mother-in-law. In the early hours of the morning Berryman brutally murdered Green and Beard by taking a hatchet to the womens' heads before stealing £200. Berryman then fled and was never found and bought to justice for his crimes. No one is sure what happened to him after this but his guilty spirit is said to haunt the building, repentant for his evil deeds. As well as his victims' screams being heard, the ghost of Agnes Beard is still seen to this day coming out of the buttery and crossing the courtyard before disappearing by the stairs that climb up to the main house.

Jenkins

The High Street in Poole runs from the middle of the town down to the quayside and is a pleasant walk through a plethora of shops and historic buildings. In the 1960s one shop in particular on the high street caused a stir when it reported to the press the various antics of a spirit named Jenkins. The shop and several of its neighbours were due to be demolished so the High Street could be completely revamped and updated and it was believed that one spirit in particular was not happy about the plans!

Management, staff and customers all witnessed objects in the shop moving, doors opening and closing on their own, cold breezes, lights flashing on and off and strange smells. The activity got so bad it is reported that customers, when seeing objects move and fly off shelves, would actually run from the shop terrified, others who stayed had to be subdued by staff. The media got involved and the apparent hauntings of this store became local news and made all the newspapers. Other shops in the vicinity also started to report activity and people actually started coming to the area to see if they could witness the sightings for themselves. Jenkins apparently performed on many occasions although when plans for the redevelopment were delayed, activity in the stores ceased as quickly as it had begun. Jenkins was described as a 'rude ghost' who seemed to enjoy pushing past people on the stairs when he passed them and generally scaring people. Those who actually claimed to see Jenkins described him as a fairly young man in a suit with a high-collared white shirt.

Many years later in the 1970s reports of experiences started to resurface and in the same shop people started reporting strange activity. Was Jenkins getting restless again? One couple believes they witnessed bottles float from the shelves and handbags hanging in midair before dropping to the floor! The original shop where this took place is no longer there and a new shop stands in its place. It appears Jenkins delayed plans but in the end was never able to stop them. Since the building of the new shop there have been no reports of the return of this rude spirit.

At night the screams of Agnes can still be heard from Scaplens Court.

Phantom Hooves

Poole, for hundreds of years, has thrived on the trade brought into and exported from the quay. The High Street provided a link directly from the quayside to the town and horses hauling ships' cargo were a common sight on the street until the late 1800s. It is thought that on a still, cold night you can still hear the clip-clop of hooves and the cries of the men as they continue to ferry their invisible goods up to the town to trade.

Phantom hooves and the sounds of a little boy sobbing may be some of the sounds experienced on the High Street.

Little Boy Child

In the late 1890s horse and carts drove at great speeds up and down the small Poole roads transporting goods to and from the port. The busy market was close by and the streets thronged with people. This tale of a haunting is a sad one and really wrenches at the heartstrings. On a busy market day a little boy aged about six was playing in the streets as normal. This day, however, was slightly different as he had with him his fifteen-week-old puppy. The little boy adored his pet but unfortunately this was to be his downfall. As a cart rumbled up the street the little dog ran out towards the cart and without thinking the small boy dashed forward to save it, putting himself in the direct path of the wagon. He was knocked down and killed instantly, the little puppy escaping unharmed.

To this day the little boy is said to wander the streets of Poole especially near the town centre (and what is now Woolworth's) looking for the little puppy he saved. He is said to appear very distressed and people are said to experience his presence not just by seeing him but sometimes by feeling a rushing sensation around them, cold breezes even in the hottest summer weather and also by hearing him sobbing. People have also reported feeling a tugging on their coats or clothing similar to the feeling of a child who is trying to get an adult's attention. When they turn to look no one is there.

It's hard not to be touched by this story and we can only hope that one day this tragic little boy will find his puppy and will be able to rest in peace.

The Antelope Hotel

This old coaching inn is situated on the High Street and is a popular place with visitors and locals standing next door to the Kings Head. The inn was built in the fifteenth century and along with the King Charles, is one of the oldest remaining public houses in Poole. In the late 1800s coaches taxied men that served the lifeboat station to the boathouse in Sandbanks on a daily basis. The Antelope has been changed considerably especially after it went under major refurbishment in 2003, however it retains much of its original charm and even some of the early building. Being so close to the quay, the High Street served as a main route for coaches to Lymington, Bristol, Weymouth, Southampton and London and the Antelope was one of the main places in Poole for the coaches to stop on their journey, offering home-cooked meals and rooms for the passengers and drivers and stabling for the horses. Like any coaching inn the Antelope has a large courtyard where at night you are still able to hear the clip-clop of hooves and the rattle of the stagecoach wheels on the cobbled ground. It is believed that on some occasions you can even hear the shout of the coachman and the crack of his whip as the coach leaves the courtyard. This busy inn is still thriving today and it appears that it is not just twenty-first-century people that are visiting either.

Old Street Lights and a Ghostly Priest

Church Street is ablaze with Georgian domestic architecture and among these buildings you can spot several medieval buildings such as the Almshouses.

Almshouses (charitable housing) were established in Britain in the 1300s to provide residences for the elderly and poor or those in certain professions and their widows. The Fraternity of St George built the St George's Almshouses in Poole in the 1400s. They were originally built to provide accommodation for the four priests serving the altars in nearby St James's church. The building was altered in 1586 following the loss of the clergy when Elizabeth I became Queen. Two very different hauntings surround this beautiful old building. On the side of the Almshouse there are small recesses in the wall originally used to house Poole's first street lights. Little candles and later oil lanterns would be placed in the recesses and they would light the nearby road enough for people to see. It is told in local legend that on very dark winter nights, these little lights can still be seen twinkling, lighting up the road next to the building. The figure of a man, dressed in black (possibly a priest) has also been seen outside the Almshouses before he turns and walks through the wall into the house. The part of the wall that he passes through does not even have a door – had there been a door there which has now been blocked up? Unfortunately we may never know.

The Kings Head and the Antelope Hotel stand side-by-side on the High Street.

The Most Haunted Building in Poole?

Known as the most haunted building in Poole, the Crown Hotel in Market Street is known to ghost hunters all over the world. This seventeenth-century coaching inn is still as splendid today as it was when it was built and attracts visitors all year round, many wishing to experience what so many others have. As part of the old town, the inn would have always been centre of the locals' lives and it appears some of those people were more reluctant to leave than others. Many of the experiences centre around the local legend that in the seventeenth century the owner of the building, embarrassed as to what people would think, hid his two deformed twins away from the public eye by chaining them in an upstairs room. Eventually, the children perished but unfortunately that is not where the tragic story ends. To cover up what he had done and hide their bodies the father is said to have then buried them under the floor in the larder. To this date, more than 400 years on, the screams of the tortured children can still be heard echoing through the hotel. Having become run down, in the 1960s a man called Alan Brown took over as

The Almshouses where the old town street lights can still be seen burning. (Heather V.)

landlord and set about a massive task of renovating and transforming it back to its former glory. During this work paranormal activity is said to have been at an all-time high as he was working on parts of the building that had not been touched since its construction. His tools, which were left in one of the outbuildings, would be found scattered all over the place. Doors would open and close on their own, lights in the cellar would flicker on and off for no apparent reason and the noise of horses' hooves could be heard during the day and the night in the hotel courtyard. In 1966 Paul Eeles, a hotel employee and his friend Malcolm Squire, reported hearing a single note being played repeatedly on the piano in a room in the hayloft that was under construction at the time. They could not understand this and on investigation found the piano closed up. Strangely however, they could still hear the note being played. As they watched, all the objects flew off the piano front of them. They had witnessed enough and left the hayloft quickly. When they went outside they turned to observe a 'fluorescent mist' float down the staircase they had just descended, cross the courtyard in front of them and disappear into the hotel. Fascinated by what they had reported, an Australian, Mr D. Browne, visited the hotel in 1967 in hopes of proving that what the men had experienced were just figments of their imagination. He planned

THIS AD 1904

THESE ALMSHOUSES
FIRST BUILT IN THE TIME OF HENRY V
AND LONG THE PROPERTY OF ST GEORGES GUILD
PASSED TO THE CROWN IN 1547
AND WERE PURCHASED FOR THE CORPORATION
IN 1550
THEY HAVE BEEN DEVOTED TO THE
USE OF THE POOR FOR 500 YEARS

The plaque on the Almshouses relating how the building has been devoted to helping the less fortunate for over 500 years.

many experiments, one of which was locking the door to the hayloft. Imagine his amazement when, after he bolted it, he saw with his own eyes the lock unbolt itself. From then on he had to take a slightly less sceptical view of what the two men had experienced the year before. In an interview afterwards with the *Dorset & Poole Herald*, Mr Browne said, 'It's the most eerie feeling I have ever had in my life.'

Between the 1970s and '80s, there were continuing reports of phenomena witnessed in the hotel including that of a local milkman who, in 1975, refused to leave milk in one part of the courtyard. He swore that on several occasions he had heard the sound of children playing right in front of him and yet he could see nothing. The landlord's wife agreed with the milkman that she too had heard this in the early morning but had just assumed it was her children. Strangely, on investigation, she had found her children were still tucked up in bed fast asleep.

In 1989 new owners Malcolm and Pat Miller had experienced more in a month than most people would encounter in a lifetime. Lights would flicker on and off all over the building but particularly in the cellar. Balls of light were seen shooting across rooms before disappearing into thin air. The couple felt icy cold blasts on their faces and an unidentified woman was seen from outside in one of the top windows of the hotel. Both the owners and some guests also witnessed a young girl in a white nightdress leaning on the banisters. In the 1990s a guest at the hotel was in his room when he noticed his door had started to rattle. As it got more violent he stepped towards it curiously but then it stopped. Seconds later he watched as the door handle twisted and the door opened. Expecting to see someone outside the door he peered out but there was no one around. He went back in to the room just in time to see a blue ball of light float around his room before drifting out of the open doorway and down the hall. Another guest had to be calmed by hotel employees when he reported standing and talking for some time to an elderly man in the men's toilet. When they had finished talking the elderly gent just vanished leaving the guest more than a little shocked!

The Crown Hotel where the ghosts of the deformed children are said to make themselves known to guests and staff.

The Former Residents of the Guildhall

The magnificent Guildhall stands at the top of Market Street. Several reports have been made over the years of ghostly soldiers seen in and around the building. There have been reports of cooking odours in areas you would not expect to smell food, and old tunes being played on a non-existent piano. People also report they feel a sense of happiness in some areas and sadness in others, a real rollercoaster of emotions. What does the building's history hide that could explain these experiences? The Guildhall was built in 1761 when two of the town's MPs, Joseph Gulston and Lt-Col. Thomas Calcraft, each pledged £750 to build a market house for Poole. Building began with the first stones being laid in the August of 1761 and the plans were designed to include a shambles, offices for Poole Corporation, courtrooms and a debating chamber. The complete cost of the building was £2,260 14s, and although money had been donated by the MPs, the mayor, George Weston, had to take out a loan to cover the excess costs incurred in the building project. Once completed, the first floor of the building was used by Poole Corporation until 1836 when it became the meeting place for the new town council who replaced the corporation. In 1932 new council buildings were opened and meetings moved from the Guildhall to the new building in the same year. The Guildhall was used for many purposes including the Poole Court of Admiralty. Admiralty courts have been held since the thirteenth century and are presided over by the Admiral of the Port, who in Poole's case was the town's mayor. This court was held in the building until it was abolished in 1835. The court dealt with legal issues concerning trade and fleets, in short everything that a domestic court would deal with, but concerned with maritime issues. Between 1819 and 1821 the Guildhall was consecrated as a parish church while the old St James's church was demolished to make way for a new larger building.

Now we come to the part in history that may explain some of the Guildhall's strange occurrences. During the Second World War it played host to American soldiers prior to the invasions of France. Records show that there was a canteen on the site, a room where more senior army personnel would meet to discuss plans, shower and washing facilities for the troops and rest areas where soldiers could relax between training. These records alone back up all of the documented sightings at the Guildhall so could it be that maybe some of our allied friends have remained here? Some of the troops' washing facilities remained in use until the 1960s when bathing cubicles on the ground floor were let out to local residents – but could you be sure you would be in there alone?

In 1972 the building was converted into the new town museum and extensive work was carried out to restore it to its original condition. Building work has long been associated with the stirring up of paranormal activity and so what else could now be roaming the halls of the Guildhall? Staff and visitors to the museum believe that the ghost of an old town clerk still wanders the building. On some days his heavy footsteps can be heard on the upper floors where he is believed to have been trapped since the day he took his own life after a long period of depression. He still walks the rooms, sad and lonely with the guilt of what he did. Some people believe that he may be trapped here eternally as this is what prevents the poor soul from moving on.

Yet another spirit may roam outside the Guildhall and it is said that if you peer at one of its walls carefully you can find a bullet mark in the stone. This marks the spot where in 1886 Alderman Horatio Hamilton (an ex-mayor of Poole) was shot by John King, a harbour pilot. The men were arguing over a boat and the dispute came to a head outside the building. King

Heavy footsteps can still be heard on the upper floor of the Guildhall. (Heather V.)

was found guilty of his crime and was sentenced to be hanged but he had a lucky escape and the people of Poole gave the killer a reprieve. It is said that Hamilton, angry that his killer escaped execution, still walks around the town, particularly outside Guildhall, looking for King so he can settle the score.

Faces in the Angel

The Angel Inn's close proximity to the Guildhall would make you presume that if it was haunted by anything then it would be by soldiers stationed there in the war or town mayors, especially when you consider that it was here that they held their election-day breakfasts. Or perhaps, the Poole Reform Party members that met at the inn in the early nineteenth century, however this does not seem to be the case at all.

In the 1980s a couple visiting Poole saw the faces of two cheeky young children, possibly a boy and a girl, staring out at them from the upstairs window of the Angel Inn in Market Street.

If you pass the Angel Inn will you be able to see the faces of the cheeky spirit children in the upstairs windows?

The children were pulling faces so the visitors pulled faces back at them and gave them a quick wave on their way past. The visitors walked between the Guildhall and the Angel to visit friends in Market Close and once they arrived at the friends' home they forgot all about the children until it was suggested that they popped out to a local pub for a drink. The local couple proposed going to the Blue Boar which would have been the closer pub but remembering the children at the window earlier in the day, the visitors suggested making their way to the Angel instead. When they arrived they could not help but look up to see if they could see the children at the window, but no one was there. Once inside, the friendly landlord and one of his bar staff greeted them and they ordered their drinks. Assuming it must be the landlord who lived upstairs, the couple commented to him how cute his children were. He looked confused; he did not have any children and there had been no children in the inn all day let alone upstairs. The couple persisted, thinking he was playing a joke on them but the member of staff was able to confirm the owner's claim that no children had been in all day. The couple, now a little shocked, asked the landlord whether the premises was known to be haunted and he said that although there were the odd strange knocks and bangs he did not know of anything unusual.

Were those seemingly innocent knocks and bangs the children playing and how many times have they been seen at the window by passers-by who presume there are children staying in the hotel? No one seems to know why they are there and belief is they are children of a former owner. Built in the late eighteenth century, this former coaching house must have seen much people traffic over the years and similarly must have had many owners, so tracking down these childrens' parents is difficult. In the late 1800s there is a record of a landlady having her two children living with her, a boy and a girl. Could these be the same children? Or are they just children of former guests? There is no notable tragedy recorded in the building involving children so it is a real mystery. If you are ever passing the Angel Inn take a quick glance up at the windows and see if you can catch sight of the cheeky pair.

Secret Tunnels

The original Blue Boar Inn stood on the quay and was built by Stephen Adey in the mid-1700s. The inn is now called the Lord Nelson and confusingly the house that Adey lived in when he ran the Blue Boar (now the Lord Nelson) is now called the Blue Boar! The ghost story surrounds Adey's old residence, the Blue Boar, located in Market Close. The Adeys were a wealthy family of wine merchants, and many generations of the family lived and worked in Poole including Adey's three sons Stephen, Thomas and William who became mariners and later took on civic duties in the town. It is Stephen and his wife that are believed to haunt the Blue Boar which once was their family home. Waitresses and staff have reported seeing dark manifestations walking across the room and subsequently through walls. There are also reports of the smell of tobacco and lavender, which are believed to signal the couple's presence in a room. When the cellars of the building were renovated it seemed to stir up the spirits and considering the trade carried on, this is probably where owner Stephen Adey would have stored the inn's alcohol. Was he innocently still trying to protect his family home and livelihood? Another sinister find was made during the repairs and that was the discovery of a blocked-up doorway. To this day no one has ever told what was found when the secret door was opened up. It could be that nothing odd was found and the doorway was just blocked up as it was not used. Legend and hearsay suggests that there

The Blue Boar – home of the Adey family in the 1700 .

was the macabre discovery of animal bones which may explain the howling of dogs that can still be heard from the cellar on some nights.

Byngley House

Byngley House and Mary Tudor Cottage were built in 1567 by Thomas Byngley, a merchant and mayor of Poole. They were originally built as a single dwelling and are some of the oldest buildings in Market Street. The street was named after the markets that thrived there in the fifteenth century when they were established by royal charter. This made the surrounding area a very affluent and desirable place to reside. Today Byngley House is the home to local businesses but its origins remain to this day. Some people who visit the house report feelings of extreme fear and subsequent suffocation and others leave one particular upstairs room feeling faint and light headed. One lady who visited the building felt as though she was being smothered by invisible hands and found it almost impossible to breathe, as though someone was holding thick cloth over her mouth and nose. These feelings disappeared when she left the building.

When the house was renovated the remains of a mummified cat nailed to the underside of the floor were found in the building. Local legend dictates that this was one way in which residents helped free themselves and their homes of evil and malevolent spirits. The cat has now been removed but has this enabled undesirable spirits to return to the house?

Captain Jolliffe

Jolliffe House stands in West Street jutting out from the town centre and is believed to be haunted by a 'teasing' ghost from whom the building takes its name. Captain Peter Jolliffe had the house built in 1712 very close to the harbour's edge. He was one of Poole's finest seafarers commanding a large fleet of ships but known locally as 'the pirate type'. Under Jolliffe House he demanded that a tunnel be built connecting directly to the quay so that his ships' goods could be hauled up the tunnels straight into his residence. The tunnels would primarily have been used to bring up the expensive French brandy he used to smuggle into Poole. The house is now used as offices for a local firm. Some of the original features still remain including a beautiful walnut staircase brought back on one of Jolliffe's ships from South Carolina.

In 2001 after many mysterious happenings at the house, the *Daily Echo* ran a story after cleaning staff were plagued by strange goings-on late at night. Doors would bang and lights would turn themselves on and off as if touched by invisible hands. The electricians were called in after one experience and they found no faults that would cause the lighting to go on and off. The sound of someone ascending the stairs has also been heard as well as creaks and bangs in empty parts of the building. One cleaner interviewed by the *Daily Echo* said 'he had found random handprints on the reception desk after he had just cleaned and polished it'. It seemed as though Captain Jolliffe enjoyed teasing the staff. On another occasion staff-training certificates hanging on the walls were all removed only to turn up approximately 40ft away on the floor. Interestingly none of the ghoulish pranks have ever been explained and even the most sceptical of staff have put the happenings down to the cheeky captain. Is Captain Jolliffe guarding a secret that keeps him grounded in the house or does he visit his former home just to play some nightly pranks on the poor unsuspecting cleaners? After capturing some French pirates and handing them over to the authorities, King William awarded Jolliffe a gold medal. The pirates were said to be carrying a large amount of treasure when they were captured, but where did it go? It is tempting to think that it may be hidden somewhere in the house and the captain is trying to protect his reputation as well as guard his ill-gotten gains. The cleaning staff are no longer scared by the cheeky pranks and now take it as part of the job.

Spectral Decor

The United Reformed church built in 1777 stands on Skinner Street. Amid housing it stands out from its surroundings and when you pass by you cannot help but stare. It feels in many

Cleaning staff at Jolliffe House have been tormented by a trick-playing spectre.

ways as though it is drawing you in. Some years ago a reporter from the *Dorset & Poole Herald* visited the church with the intention of writing a story about its history. He entered the building and wrote about its old-fashioned high pews and magnificent brass lamps. Before the story was published he revisited the church – however this time things were completely different. Confused by what he had seen, he spoke to vicar and was shocked to learn that what he had in fact seen on his last visit, merely weeks before, was the decor of the church more than 100 years ago. The pews, lamps and similar adornments had been removed from the church to make way for more modern furniture and fittings. Understandably this left the reporter and the vicar somewhat shocked. Unable to speak directly, was this the building's way of giving a little bit of its history to the reporter? To back this up, people living around the church have reported seeing the glow of old-fashioned lights in the church in the late evening when the church is empty and has been locked up for the night. The lights appear to be on for sometimes only a matter of minutes, before dying out and returning the church to darkness. In the 1980s one of the residents of Skinner Street approached the vicar at the time and asked him about these strange lights. The vicar apparently laughed knowingly saying he was not surprised they had been seen but assured the man that he was the only key holder and that the building had been empty on the particular night in question. Another local man reported walking by the church on his way home from a night out one December night. It was approximately midnight and he described the church as being bathed in an orangey-yellow light. He stood and watched for a few seconds and the light seemed to fade, again returning the church to darkness. In early 2000 two members of a local paranormal team spent two hours outside the church and although they did not observe any lights coming from within the building, they did report that at 12.10 a.m. the church appeared to be bathed in a calming orange glow but only for a matter of minutes

The United Reformed church on Skinner Street, where lights can be seen even when the building is empty.

CHAPTER TWO

POOLE:
PARISHES AND SUBURBS

The Haunted Island

Within Poole Harbour lie eight islands of varying sizes, the largest being Brownsea Island now owned by the National Trust. The island is most famous for being the location of Lt-Gen. Baden-Powell's first experimental Scout camp for boys in 1907 although the island's history goes back centuries and can be somewhat regarded as chequered.

Brownsea Island's first known inhabitant was a hermit in the seventh century who lit beacons on the north shores to guide ships safely into the harbour. Little is known about this man who lived away from the mainland in isolation but he is said to still haunt the island to this day. Most of the land on the island is now a nature reserve and is kept unspoilt but yet on some nights, especially when the weather is poor and visibility is bad, boats and their crews coming into the harbour have reported seeing flaming beacons on the shore. Once they have passed the island, crews report these spectral flames just disappearing. Is the hermit still to this day keeping sea craft from danger and guiding boats safely into the harbour?

Henry VIII, England's second Tudor monarch, fortified the island when he built the castle; since then the building has changed hands many times. One owner is said to have committed suicide in one of the ground-floor rooms and is said to still roam the corridors. He has been seen on many an occasion by staff and visitors. A lady who worked on the island reported that she and a colleague were in their room on the ground floor at approximately 11 p.m. when one of them saw a large black-hooded figure bending over her bed. Obviously the women were terrified and did what many of us suspect we would do if we saw a ghost and pulled their bedclothes over their heads and remained that way until dawn, too scared to look out. Could this have been the ghost of the owner that took his own life?

In the 1890s, after the installation of electricity, the castle caught fire and was only ever partially rebuilt, losing much of its original Tudor charm. In the late 1920s a Mrs Bonham-Christie purchased the island at auction and banned visitors after a forest fire destroyed nearly half of the land. Her ideas to turn the island into a bird sanctuary were noble, however with little help the island soon became overgrown and the castle fell into disrepair. Her family, recognising she was having problems coping, moved her off the island though this was believed to be against her wishes. She passed away the day she was moved. When she died in the 1960s the castle was in ruins and the National Trust purchased the island, helping rebuild the castle, surviving cottages and St Mary's church. A ghostly lady matching Mrs Bonham-Christie's description has been seen by many visitors in the grounds around the castle. The spirit of the lady is said to just stand looking out at the sea and does not interact with anyone that witnesses her. A photograph was also taken in May 2003 which showed the face of a woman at one of the windows of the house. On closer inspection of the snapshot it was described as having, 'remarkable likeness to Mrs Bonham-Christie'. Has the spirit of this old lady returned to the place she loved so much and was forced to leave against her wishes?

Mystical Music

If you cross the bridge at the quay you arrive in the parish and suburb of Poole called Hamworthy. Once a Roman settlement called Moriconium, it was a thriving area that made use of the natural harbour for transport and trade. It prospers now as a mix between industrial and residential Poole. With a population of over 14,000 it is an increasingly popular place to reside with houses in close proximity to Poole but without the town-centre price tag. Hamworthy has changed over the years and little remains of its Roman past. However if you listen carefully on some nights you can apparently still hear the spirits of the Roman inhabitants. If you stand on the shore you can hear on the wind the solemn sounds of a tuba. It is said to be very sad music and makes anyone that hears it very sombre. As the Romans buried their dead near water it is possible this is funeral music. Unlike the modern-day tuba, its Roman predecessor was a straight, bronze trumpet-like instrument, sometimes up to 1.3m long. It made a very distinctive sound and was higher in pitch than today's tuba which is probably why even those who understand instruments can not identify what they are hearing.

The Spirits of Lake House

Set in a wooded area of Hamworthy is Lake House. It now serves as the officers' mess of the Poole Royal Marines but this beautiful house with its stunning interior tells a tragic and macabre tale of desperation and sadness that you cannot imagine by just looking at it. It was built by William Cecil in 1903 on land owned by Lord Rockley although there is documentary evidence that there has been a house on this site since at least the 1800s. The Rockley initials can still be seen over the front entrance to the property but sadly this is where the house's tragic story begins as William Cecil hanged himself for reasons that are still not clear.

In 1911 after Cecil's death the house was purchased by Lt-Col. the Hon. Henry Christian Guest. He was the son of the first Baron of Wimborne who owned a large portion of the Hamworthy land. Guest, an army man, lived in the house with his family and served his country extensively especially in the Second World War when he spent months away from the family home. His wife was said to be of a depressive disposition and the long periods of separation from her husband eventually resulted in her shooting herself during a particularly deep bout of

A steamship in the entrance of Poole Harbour, 1910.

depression, adding another chapter to the tragic story. In 1919 Capt. Charles Gardiner purchased the house with his wife Clara. Despite extensive plans for the extension of his lake shipyard, Gardiner, an ex-army officer of the tank regiment, was declared bankrupt shortly after buying the property. Bailiffs ready to take possession of the house were stalled when Clara died of cancer. Old Laws prohibit bailiffs entering a house when there is a body laid at rest and so Gardiner saw this as a way of securing his home. He kept the mummified body of Clara in one of the bedrooms in the house until 1921 when she was finally laid to rest at Hamworthy Parish Cemetery. Gardiner died in 1930 in Greenwich. There are two coffins carved in relief outside the room where Clara was kept which mark the part the couple played in the history of Lake House. It was eventually bought by the Ministry of Defence in 1949 and turned into the officers' mess that you see today. So is Lake House haunted by the spirits of such a colourful but sad past? Its current residents would have you believe it is and it is hard to not give credence to a story when told to you by those who have seen more things in this world than the man in the street can imagine. Marines regularly report feeling the presence of a lady in the house with them, whom they believe to be the restless spirit of Henry Guest's wife. The marines think she still wanders the house looking for her husband, the man she missed so much it drove her to take her own life – does she still feel at home here with the men that she would have been used to mixing with? Cold spots are experienced on warm days, several men can feel her presence when she is around and will suddenly stop what they are doing and acknowledge her. Invisible feet are heard pacing the floors and a general sense of sadness and oppression is felt in some rooms when normally they are known to have a light and carefree atmosphere. Some of the marines are genuinely frightened by her sudden eerie presence and again you have to remember that these are men that are not easily frightened!

Haunted Manor

The wonderful manor house, later to be known as the Rectory, was built in the 1600s and is famed for being one of the first brick-built houses in the county. It belonged to the staunch Roman Catholic Carew family and has seen many notable guests over the years. According to local legend Cromwell stayed there when Corfe Castle was being stormed and many of the injured men were brought back to the house. During the Napoleonic Wars the manor became the headquarters of the British Army Southern Command and the Duke of Wellington is also believed to have visited. During the eighteenth century the house was acquired by the Lord of Canford Manor and by the nineteenth century had been converted into three separate homes. In 1826 when the church was built, the Lord of Canford Manor gave the house to the Parish of Hamworthy to be used as a rectory. Unusually before he bestowed it he had the staircase removed and installed in Canford Manor. The Rectory played an important role in the community. Sadly over the following years the house fell into disrepair and at one point was even considered for demolition until the Department of Environment stepped in and announced the need to preserve it. The house was sold to a local couple in 1980 and they undertook the massive task of renovating it. In 1997 it was sold, fully restored, to a young family who, despite the tales that it has a rather strange ghost, have never experienced anything paranormal. Oliver Knott's book *Tales of Dorset* describes how the house, having been returned to the Carew family, was witness to a very strange love affair. The lady of the manor was besotted with her husband's eccentric but handsome cousin. They had a long illicit affair and she was entranced by his 'devil may care' attitude to life. He would visit her at night and would signal his arrival by whistling in a very unusual manner. He had the ability to mimic animals and birds and would use a bird whistle to attract the attention of his lover who would then sneak out of the house to meet him in the grounds. His impersonation of animals went a little further than just his whistling and he was often said to disguise himself in animal skins so his friends would not recognise him.

The story goes that on one occasion he took this too far and killed a man, skinned him and then wore the skin to impersonate the dead man! During the affair the husband of the lady grew suspicious and one night when he discovered them in each other's arms he shot them both. He proceeded to dump his cousin's body in the pond and took his wife's lifeless body back into the house. This series of events is said to have been the turning point at which the Carew family lost control of the house and enabled it to be acquired by the Lord of Canford Manor. For years after it is said that the cousin haunted the house and that his unusual whistles could still be heard calling for his secret lover's attention. As previously mentioned, more recent owners of the property have not reported any activity in or around the house, yet with such a bird-like whistle, maybe they have indeed heard him and just not realised it!

The quay in the early 1900s.

The People's Park

Poole Park since its opening in 1890 has been a popular place for locals and tourists to visit. Situated remarkably close to the town centre it boasts picturesque boating lakes, play areas, a rose garden and a rich habitat for many species of birds including its most famous residents, Canada geese. The park was built on land donated by the then Lord Wimborne and was opened with a special ceremony in 1890 by the Prince of Wales, Albert Edward, eleven years before he became king.

Many a haunting tale can be told about Poole Park, in fact a book itself could be written just containing stories and legends from the its hundred years. I have chosen a few of the more unusual ones to whet the appetite.

Gemma and Jonathan

This story centres on a tree near the centre gates of the park. A local spiritual medium, David Austin of Parkstone told me the story of Gemma and Jonathan. For years growing up he lived

The Victorians enjoyed leisure time in Poole Park.

near the park and as a child aged ten in the 1980s played there most days after school with his friends. This is where he met Gemma and Jonathan. The pair were twins and wore funny clothes that David was not familiar with. Jonathan always wore braces and a cotton shirt with a necktie and Gemma always wore the same pretty lemon dress with a big white frilly collar. They were nice children and David believed their attire meant they were from the more affluent part of town. Nearly everyday David would meet the pair at the tree closest to the gates and they would play hide and seek and sometimes sit and talk for hours. Gemma and Jonathan loved listening to the stories David told of his father's old cars, what homework he had that night and what his pet dog Rancher has done at the weekend. David believed that the twins had a rather boring life and did not have had any friends as they rarely had stories to tell apart from talking about their mother Winifred. He often invited them to visit his house and to meet his family but the twins always declined saying they were not allowed to leave the park until their mother arrived to take them home. One day he took his friend Peter to meet them. They waited in the usual place at the usual time but for the first time, Gemma and Jonathan did not arrive. Peter became bored and decided to leave. It was then, out of nowhere, David said he saw Gemma and Jonathan appear by the tree. Not really understanding fully what he was seeing David ran home and told his mother. She told David the story of two local twins that in 1920 on a cold winter's day had been left in the park. The couple waited patiently for their mother to return as they had been told never to leave the park without their mother's permission; however she never returned. The twins huddled under a tree but due to the harsh winter weather they died of exposure and their lifeless bodies were found at sunrise the next morning. David being scared by this story, refused to return to the park. It was not until later in life when he was developing his mediumship

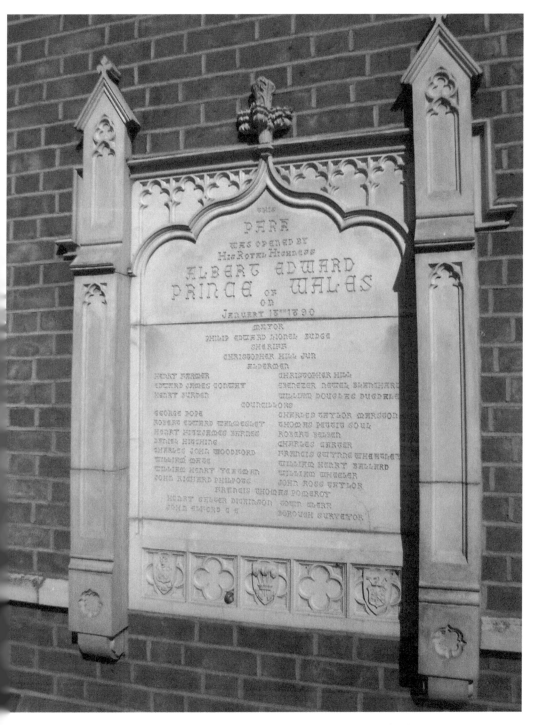

The plaque at the entrance to Poole Park commemorating its opening by the Prince of Wales.

abilities that he returned to the park to privately thank Gemma and Jonathan for their help. If they had not appeared to him he believes he would never have pursued mediumship in any way. When he returned to the park he could sense them around and believed he could hear Gemma giggling but sadly was not able to see them like he had done before. Are these two unfortunate children set to wander the park forever, waiting for their mother to collect them? David hopes they have in fact moved on and that they maybe just come back occasionally to visit the park where they spent their last night.

An Old Sea Dog, a Lady in Black and Phantom Troops!

In the centre of the park is a beautiful memorial to Earl Mountbatten of Burma, Admiral of the Fleet. There are two haunting tales that originate around this splendid memorial.

Born in 1900, Louis Mountbatten served in the navy in both world wars. In the Second World War he commanded the destroyer HMS *Kelly* until it was sunk near Crete when he was appointed captain of HMS *Illustrious*. After the war he was a major figure working for the independence of India and Pakistan and was nominated for the positions of the last viceroy and first governor-general of the newly independent India by then Prime Minister Clement Attlee.

In July 1922 he married Edwina Cynthia Annette Ashley and lived in Broadlands House in Romsey, however Edwina died in North Borneo in February 1960 aged just fifty-eight. The Earl Mountbatten died on 27 August 1979 when he was killed by an IRA bomb. The 50lb bomb was fixed to his sailing boat while he was on holiday in County Sligo in the Republic of Ireland. His death was mourned all over the country especially in the southern counties where he held a strong association. After his funeral in London he was brought home and was buried in Romsey.

The first story is that Earl Mountbatten, so touched by this show of affection for him, haunts the park. He has apparently been seen by visitors standing by the memorial, in his full navy uniform, looking out to sea. Little has been documented about this sighting and so there is not much to go on. It is equally as possible it could be an old sea captain from Poole possibly revisiting his old haunt.

A more documented haunting of the memorial is that of a ghostly lady dressed in black. She has been seen sitting on the wall surrounding the pillar, weeping quietly. Many people have seen her including a retired police sergeant and so credence to his story is hard to ignore. The lady, dressed in black, together with a veil, is seen sitting facing the pillar where the plaque is mounted. She is obviously distressed when she appears to passers-by and many offer her kind words but she takes no comfort from them and makes no apparent effort to communicate, continuing to sob profusely into her white handkerchief. Those who see her report overwhelming feelings of sadness or distressing feelings of guilt when they are near her. As she makes no effort to respond, people feel they have no choice but to leave her alone in her sorrow. When they turn to check as they are leaving, the figure has disappeared leaving them shocked and confused. Again, as with any sighting there is always much speculation as to who the pitiful woman is. Many believe she is the Earl's wife Edwina. Having passed herself so young, it is believed that she is still searching for her husband. Maybe the Earl, having lost his wife many years before his own death, came to terms with his loss and has been able to move on. Considering the circumstances of her husband's death and the fact that she passed away in Borneo, maybe she is

The lady in black is seen sitting on the wall by this memorial to the Earl Mountbatten of Burma.

Phantom troops surround this water's-edge monument to the men and women who lost their lives in the First and Second World Wars.

still trapped in our world searching for her partner. The most impressive piece of information is that the same figure has been seen in Romsey, County Sligo and other places connected to the Earl including Borneo and India where views on the paranormal are very different to ours. Does this lonely widow travel the length and breadth of England and possibly the world searching for her departed Louis?

A third haunting surrounds the war memorial on the waterfront. Apparently on some nights it is surrounded by khaki-clad soldiers who are standing to attention but with their heads bowed as if in mourning and paying their respects. There are never more than seven of them, so whether this is significant or not, I do not know, however they are only ever seen from afar and people tend to see them, look away, realise what they have seen, but when they look back the soldiers have disappeared. Some speculation has been made as to whether they are American due to their strong presence in Poole in the Second World War. The colour of their uniforms would support this theory though no one knows why they appear in the park.

A peaceful scene in Poole Park where the atmosphere is said to change at night.

Phantom Rower

For hundreds of years a wide stretch of the harbour channel separated Poole and Swanage. The nearest crossing point was between Sandbanks and Shell Bay but the dangerous currents always meant that the trip was a treacherous one. Today Poole is connected to Swanage by the 'floating bridge' which carries thousands of cars, pedestrians and bicycles every year. The channel could not be crossed in such luxury 100 years ago. In the early 1900s a rowing-boat service operated on this stretch of water but was dependent upon tidal flow. In 1908 James Harvey, a local man, started operating a motorboat service for people wanting to cross to Swanage – his helmsmen are said to haunt the waters although their names are not known. The floating bridge is a chain ferry and therefore can not drastically change its course. On a quiet night in the summer of 2004 few people were on the ferry. Even though the crossing takes a matter of minutes, pedestrians may walk on the viewing gallery while they cross and this is what a particular pair of walkers did that night on their trip back to Shell Bay.

The Bramble Bush Bay floating bridge connecting Studland to Poole.

It was a warm night and the moon shone down on the water. All of a sudden one of the walkers panicked as he saw in the moonlight a man in a small wooden rowing boat crossing the path of the ferry. He ran down the steps and up to the gallery on the other side of the boat to see if the rower had managed to get through safely but to his surprise there was no rowing boat to be seen. He waited another minute but nothing materialised. Is this phantom rower still making his trips across from Sandbanks to Shell Bay completely oblivious that he is crossing the ferry's path? Maybe if you wander down to the shore you will be able to see the lonely rower. If not it is also said that on some nights, in the dead of night, you can still hear the buzz of James Harvey's little motorboat running backwards and forwards across the water as he carries on doing the job he loved.

Spooky Voices

The Haven Hotel has been at the southernmost tip of Sandbanks (and the Poole peninsula) for over 100 years. It is a beautiful and somewhat exclusive hotel where people can stay with the sea literally lapping at their door. Before the hotel was built it was used as a look-out point due

An aerial view of the Sandbanks peninsula and the Haven Hotel.

to its multi-angle views of the entrance into the harbour. A building is thought to have been on this site for 250 years though what kind of building it was and what it was used for is unknown. Its stark white exterior makes it stand out from everything around it and guests that have stayed there, repeatedly book year after year. It is hard to imagine the amount of well-known people that have stayed at the Haven Hotel in its lifetime, however one particular guest may have never left.

In 1897 the hotel was the site of some very interesting experiments. Guglielmo Marconi was an Italian electrical engineer and inventor, best known for his work in the development of the radiotelegraph system. Although he cannot claim to have invented wireless radio, as Nikola Tesla's patent was upheld in a US court in 1943 making him the official inventor, Marconi is probably the most well-known name with regards to his work in testing the idea. After transmitting wirelessly 14 miles with his catchphrase 'Are you ready?' he wanted to better this and chose Poole for his next set of experiments. The Haven Hotel was chosen as the site for one such experiment. Marconi arrived in 1897 and after setting up his equipment at the hotel, he was able to receive the radio signals sent from Alum Bay on the Isle of Wight over 20 miles away. After much work in the radio industry including designing and providing safety radios for sea vessels (including the one that enabled the crew on the *Titanic* to radio the RMS *Carpathia* for

The Haven Hotel where Marconi's message can still be heard.

help) he died in 1937 in Rome aged sixty-three. So does Marconi still visit the hotel? According to one ex-hotel employee, he is sure he does.

In 1977 an employee called John worked nights in the hotel. Although he would not usually be in charge of answering any phone calls, if no one else was around then he would happily man the telephone. At approximately 3.30 a.m. the phone in the hotel's reception began to ring so John made his way to it from the dining room. He answered it in his usual polite manner but all he could hear on the end of the line was a lot of buzzing and interference. He continued to listen and very faintly, amid all the background noise he heard the words 'Are you ready?' A little confused, John hung up the phone and a couple of seconds later picked it up again. He listened and it was exactly the same thing with a distant voice calling 'Are you ready?' Eager to get on with his work he hung up the phone and thought nothing more of it. It was not until about three weeks later when John was talking to a friend that he was made aware of Marconi's famous words. Was Marconi making his presence known eighty years on, maybe the best way he knew how, through technology?

The badge of the Poole Pirates Speedway Team, 1960.

Gone to the Dogs

Poole Stadium is not only home to the local greyhound racing circuit but also to the Poole Pirates who are one of the country's largest speedway teams. For years it has been a popular place for an evening's entertainment and race nights bring out the regulars who have been going to the stadium for years, as well as people visiting for the first time. It stands close to Holes Bay and on its approach it does not look very old or even very spooky, however when you look around you see how the structure and design give hints to its age. The stadium opened its gates to speedway fans on 26 April 1948 when over 7,000 post-war locals packed the Wimborne Road side, each paying the equivalent of 11p each for an evening's entertainment and first ever speedway race at the stadium. Access was gained through the pavilion turnstiles at the front of the stadium – the original turnstiles are still in place to this day. This building is listed and now houses the stadium offices and reception. A wonderful new building has been added to its south side to take the increase in the number of people visiting. Although the original building is now listing to the west it is still evident where the original entrance is. Poole Football Club fans

The old entrance to Poole Stadium, now offices, where staff sense being watched.

would also have used the entrance, though due to financial difficulties the club had to leave the stadium and relocate. Stadia UK now own the stadium and there is an event at the venue most nights. In common with many of the houses in Wimborne Road, it is built on Victorian landfill site and general manager Shaun Spencer-Perkins admits, 'The reception staff are particularly twitchy over paranormal stuff'. Staff feel as though they are being watched and cold spots come and go with no sensible explanation. Objects also get moved around. Is someone playing games with them? The ghost of an older gentleman in a white coat with dark hair has also been seen standing on the track late at night. It is only when he is approached that he disappears. Was he one of the stadium stewards, who would have worn white to make him more visible, returning to the job he loved?

Phantom Footballer

If you walk around the side of Poole Stadium you arrive at a hidden gate which gives a sense of stepping back in time. The hidden entrance still proudly displays the 'Poole Town Football

Poole Stadium's new entrance.

Club' sign from the days when the team used to play at the Wimborne Road ground. The club was founded in 1880 but the sign is old and the land, out of sight, is not in keeping with the rest of the stadium's standards. It is here that the apparition of a young footballer is seen dressed in team colours red and white. Those who see this apparition are not disturbed by it as they believe they are just watching a boy kicking a ball about. It is not until he looks up, notices them and then walks through the closed door of the grandstand admissions entrance that they realise what they have indeed seen. The young footballer is described as in his late teens, possibly early twenties and short in stature. The only unusual thing they do notice about him is how extraordinarily pale he is – his face is ashen white and a stark contrast to his dark hair. The apparition seems quite recent and it makes you wonder whether this is the spirit of a young local fan rather than a player. This theory would be backed up by the report from one person that he was also sporting a club scarf, something a player would not be wearing. Poole FC played at the stadium between 1933 and 1994 and built it as their home ground for sixty-one years, only leaving because of financial problems. If memories were recorded in the fabric of a building then this should be a prime example as thousands of fans would have passed through these gates to watch their team play. For hundreds of years people have believed that

The old Poole FC entrance to Poole Stadium where the lone fan is still seen waiting.

when you pass you return to the place you love and were most happy and for one young fan this certainly seems to be the case. Even though his team no longer play there, it is obviously somewhere he remembers with fondness.

Railway Ghosts

Poole railway station was built on wasteland on the edge of the town close to Holes Bay and the original station was opened in December 1872. In 1888 a direct route to London via Bournemouth was opened. The original station was built of brick with a wooden roof, however it has been rebuilt twice since to keep up with modern styles as far as possible. The building that stands there today is much more futuristic and has an innovative suspended vaulted roof.

Many visitors have reported seeing the fleeting figure of a woman in a long white dress. No one knows why this woman haunts the station or any details about her. She appears both day and night and one person who I spoke to, who had witnessed this spectral lady, said she appears very quickly and seems to be in a terrible hurry to get somewhere. Other reports give a vague description of her as dressed in clothes of the Victorian era, in her early twenties with dark hair tied up on her head and wearing white gloves. It has been suggested the outfit is not unlike a Victorian wedding gown. Why is this young bride doomed to spend her days at the railway station?

If you follow the track towards Poole it takes you through the town itself and actually crosses the High Street. The original level crossing is still in use to this day and anyone that shops in Poole regularly will be used to having their shopping trip interrupted by the familiar bell to signal the lowering of the gates and the imminent arrival of a train. Until 1977 the original wooden gates were being used, however laws determining level-crossing safety ensured these were changed with modern and safer lifting barriers controlled by CCTV. In the 1940s when the wooden gates were still in use many signal operators at the crossing witnessed the figure of a man standing on the track, staring up the line just after they had closed the gates and returned to their boxes. Alarmed, the operators would go back down to the track to move the man on before the train arrived, only to find that there was no one there. The man was seen so often by crossing staff that he was given the nickname of 'Crossing Cuthbert'. He was only ever seen from the signal box and had always disappeared by the time the signalman got to the track. I believe he was last seen in 1949, since then he has never appeared again. What happened to Crossing Cuthbert that last night?

Chattering at the Village Hall

Canford Cliffs village is often considered to be the 'Beverley Hills' of Poole. Many of the houses are substantial, the cars expensive and the people well dressed but under this façade is a thriving village with a relatively small population of 1,900-2,000. This village has a real sense of purpose and community and many people choose to live here in their retirement years. The 'Cliffs of Canford' were once the property of Lord Wimborne and formed part of his Canford Estate. In the 1880s some of his land was sold to a consortium that set up the Canford Cliffs Estate Co. The plan was to build houses centrally to form a small village. By the 1920s most of the plots had been built over and a village community was starting to take shape including the erection of a village hall in Ravine Road. With the lifting of post-war building restrictions in the early 1950s, remaining plots were divided, larger houses redeveloped and new blocks of flats introduced.

Throughout this time the village hall acted as a community centre, somewhere for the people of the village to gather, and in 1925 the Canford Women's Institute started to meet there on a regular basis. Within a year of the group forming, membership had risen to over 130 and the women used the hall to talk about events they were planning which included dances and bridge tournaments. The group stopped meeting there in February 2005 as membership numbers had declined due to the popularity of the WI in other areas, too many groups having been formed locally and in inadvertent competition with each other. Before the final meeting and during the hall's renovations, records were found that could explain some of the strange occurrences.

Poole central railway station.

The hall now plays host to many local groups and societies and some members have noticed strange goings-on in the building. Even when it was locked up, lights could be seen coming from within and when people were there alone they reported hearing the sound of chattering voices, ghostly laughing and old scratchy gramophone music as well as the aroma of scented tobacco smoke even though smoking was not allowed in the hall. The curtains appeared to open and close by themselves, and the figure of a lady in a red dress with a black fur jacket has been seen at the back of one of the rooms. She appeared to another lady who was preparing to lock up and was doing her final checks to make sure everything was in order. The figure was so solid that the woman thought there was someone in the hall with her but immediately noticed her dated dress and fur coat. She was also smoking a long cigarette and the woman's first thought was that smoking was not permitted and had not been for some time. When she said 'hello' the ghostly woman in red smiled and disappeared. The records that were found were from the Women's Institute in 1925 and charted their aims for the year – aims that included entertaining needy children at Christmas and discussions about whether the women should be allowed to smoke at meetings. It seems this ghostly lady may have voted in favour of smoking during meetings! So do

Canford Cliffs Village Hall where the original ladies of the Women's Institute can still be heard chatting.

some of the women that attended those meetings still remain in the hall today? Is it their voices chattering and is it their dancing music that can still be heard more than eighty years on?

Old Sea Witch Hotel

The hotel, situated on the hill in Canford Cliffs village, overlooks the type of boats it took its name from in Poole Harbour. The popular Loch Fyne Restaurant and Milsoms Hotel now own the site formerly occupied by the Sea Witch and the hotel was completely revamped but most importantly left standing. A couple of years before it was redeveloped, it was a small, thriving family-run hotel before its sudden decline into disrepair. A Mr Carr then purchased the property and due to its bad state, closed it down immediately, with plans to have it demolished to make way for new blocks of flats. This created a local uproar from its Canford Cliff neighbours and during the battle that ensued the hotel was left standing empty. During the period it was unoccupied many reports were made that lights had been seen in the abandoned hotel that

Loch Fyne Restaurant which used to be the Old Sea Witch Hotel.

made it look as though it was still occupied and the face of a non-existent guest was seen at the hotel's windows. Before any hotel was built on this site, it was occupied by small outbuildings rumoured to be the haunt of the local pirate gangs.

Canford Cliffs, with its magnificent views of the harbour entrance, was once a popular haunt for smugglers from where they could keep an eye on the comings and goings into Poole. The blue lady was a popular spectral resident of the old hotel, one ex-employee told me. She could be seen, or at least felt, in many of the rooms and a dramatic drop in temperature signified her presence which lead her to be nicknamed the blue lady. She was also said to be seen on the lower floors and guests would often feel a strong, cold breeze pass them even on the warmest day. Objects would move and overnight she particularly enjoyed rearranging the cutlery that had been laid out the previous evening for breakfast. Some of the staff did not like visiting several of the rooms and in a few areas of the hotel they would only venture in pairs as doors would open and close on their own and strange noises appeared to come from nowhere. The blue lady's face was also seen at one of the upstairs windows looking out towards the harbour. Local rumour has it that when the plans were put in place for the hotel to be demolished she made herself known by lighting up rooms in the hotel to make it look lived in. Some say she was the mistress of a pirate and was in fact lighting the lamps to show her lover that she was home waiting for him. Others take a much more down to earth view of the story, believing in fact that it was merely the reflection of car headlights creating an illuminating glow in the old windowpanes, but that surely does not explain the other activity at the hotel.

Thankfully the old Sea Witch was never demolished to make way for flats and the hotel was restored to more than its former glory. Does the blue lady still haunt this hotel? Maybe while you are eating there on a hot summer's evening and you feel an icy-cold blast of air that comes out of nowhere, you will know for sure.

The Lonely Headless Hitcher

Nearly every town or city in the country has a tale of a headless ghost and Poole is no different though this story is not as well known as most 'headless' tales and it is not the usual 'headless highwayman' or a 'headless lady'. De Mauley Road, named after Baron De Mauley of Canford, is a beautiful, solely residential road situated in Canford Cliffs. One of the road's residents, a wealthy retired banker came forward with his story – a story that until this day has remained untold.

Early one morning Mr X (to keep his anonymity), who was in his early sixties, was leaving home to collect his brother from the airport. The morning started like any other but is one that he assures me will stick in his mind forever but possibly for all the wrong reasons. He backed his car out of his drive and got out to close the large gates. It was a dark, winter morning and as Mr X turned back to his car he noticed a young man dressed in a grey jogging suit walking down the road. Glancing at his watch, surprised that someone would be out as early as he was, Mr X passed the end of the drive and bid the stranger a good morning. The young walker did not respond and just continued walking past. A little disgruntled at his ignorance in not returning the gesture, Mr X locked the gates and returned to his car. He started making his journey down the road when he noticed the young man ahead of him who was waving violently and desperately seemed to be trying to attract the attention of the driver. Slowing down immediately, thinking that the stranger was in some sort of trouble, Mr X then wound down his window as he approached but as he got nearer, the once solid figure of the man seemed to fade and when he stopped by the area where the young man was standing he disappeared completely. Assuming his mind was playing tricks on him, Mr X rubbed his eyes in disbelief and then turned to his left and nearly hit the roof of the car in horror; sitting next to him was the young man. He only saw him for a couple of seconds but the most disturbing thing was that he appeared headless. It was definitely the man he had seen earlier as he wore the same jogging suit, but his image soon faded and this former banker, a sensible, logical man was left terrified and bewildered by what he had just seen. He reversed the car as quickly as possible back to his house and went inside and made himself a very strong cup of coffee. When he had stopped shaking he made his way to collect his brother from the airport but never spoke a word to anyone about what he had seen. Who was this strange hitcher? No reports have ever been made before of seeing him in De Mauley Road and there are certainly no

De Mauley Road in the pretty village of Canford Cliffs.

records of any headless bodies being found there. It is a real mystery. The stranger seemed to be dressed in modern attire (a jogging suit and white trainers narrows him down to the late 1900s) however there is no history to back up the sighting. This is why the man feared to tell his story, worrying about his good name in the community and that he would be classed as 'a bit mad'. He no longer lives on the road but is still an active and well-known member of the community which is why he wishes to remain anonymous. I thank him for this account as without it, the story of the headless hitcher would not be known and maybe this will enable others who have witnessed seeing the hitcher to come forward – maybe then the story this young man is obviously trying to tell, can be told.

Smugglers' Cliff

Running along the cliff tops as its name suggests, connecting Poole and Bournemouth is Cliff Drive. Although a fairly recently developed area some properties date back to 1890. It is also

The view from Cliff Drive overlooking the entrance to the harbour and Old Harry Rocks in the distance. It is easy to see why smugglers and pirates would have used this spot as a look out.

a natural beauty spot from where you can gaze out at Bournemouth to the east and Poole Harbour entrance to the west. If the view is clear you can even see Old Harry Rocks (named after the legendary Poole pirate, Harry Paye) straight ahead of you. The view is spectacular and it is easy to see why properties on this road command some of the higher-end sale prices in the area. It is not busy even in the tourist season. At night the road takes on a darker feel where people feel the need to look behind them as they walk, and on a murky night the dark sea provides a cavernous backdrop as though looking out at nothing. If it were not for the lights of Bournemouth and the Purbecks it would feel as though you were at the end of the world, with nothing but blackness ahead. On a clear night you can see the twinkling of boat lights on the horizon making their way to and from the harbour, and it then becomes apparent why this area would have been the best look-out point to the sea in the whole of the county. You can see for miles and this would have been a great asset to sailors and more importantly smugglers who wanted to keep a close eye on what ships were arriving at the port. Much of the land would have been privately owned at this point so coming here to spy on the sea would have had to been done sneakily so as not to arouse suspicion and a viewpoint would have to be gained

Hunger Hill Junction at the back of the old town.

from other areas on the cliff top. All this could very well explain the sightings of strange men acting suspiciously on this road. If you are ever there, keep an eye out for them. They hide in the shadows and apparently their whistling can be heard on the wind. Are these the spirits of some of the most notorious smugglers in the south?

Ghoulish Beggars

On the main route out of the old town you have to travel along West Street which today is a main carriageway. Though this road has existed for over 400 years in the eighteenth century it was smaller, much less busy and housed a particular type of Poole resident. It is the spirits of these residents that are said to still roam the area, particularly a stretch known as 'Hunger Hill'.

In 1739 Thomas Missing provided £500 for a workhouse to be built on West Street. In 1777 a report recorded that, 'St James workhouse in the County Town of Poole had accommodation for up to eighty inmates'. 'Inmates' suggests the residents felt as though the workhouse was more like a prison than a home. Workhouses were primarily set up to house the poor, the sick,

What is left of the original workhouse building in St Mary's Road.

the mentally ill and the disabled Not all had to go there as some could claim what was known as 'parish relief', a small sum of money from their local parish, to help them stay in their own home, if they had one. For those that had no home, conditions in the workhouses were often poor and disease was rife due to poor sanitation. Today a lot of people are unaware of the history of the workhouse on West Street as it has long since been demolished to make way for urban development in the town – however, are the people of the workhouse left to wander the streets once more?

A particularly chilling report is one from a man who walked past the Hunger Hill junction every evening on his way home from work. One evening he was walking from the old town and as he approached an area by some old gravestones in a small area of a park, he always felt as though he was being watched. It was dusk and the light was fading but he could still see around him and ignored the feeling of being watched and continued on his way. Suddenly he was approached by an elderly man who held out his deformed hands in a cup shape towards him. The beggar did not look the man in the face but he could see he was unshaven, with dark, matted hair and sores on his face; he also smelt as though he had not washed for months and the stench of urine was almost unbearable. The beggar ignored all the efforts the man made to move him on. Desperate to get rid of him, the man pulled a 50p piece out of his pocket and dropped it into the beggar's dirty, twisted hands. To the man's shock the coin dropped straight to the floor. Thinking the beggar had dropped it accidentally the man bent down to retrieve it to give it back to him. When he stood up the figure had gone. Looking around he could see no sign of the beggar and he simply knew he could not have moved so fast. In disbelief at what he had just experienced and thinking no one would believe him, the man made his way home.

In the nineteenth century Britain's population was increasing rapidly and something needed to be done to deal with the rising levels of poverty. The Poor Law Act of 1834 allowed parishes to form unions with other parishes in their area, enabling them to build a bigger workhouse in the centre of each union. Now if people wanted to claim parish relief they could only do it by going into a workhouse. This was seen as a way of monitoring the poor in each union, especially the ones who were considered 'too drunk or too lazy' to look after themselves. The Poole Poor Union was formed on 2 October 1835 and consisted of eight parishes: Poole St James, Canford Magna, Hamworthy, Kinson, Longfleet, Lytchett Matravers, Lytchett Minster and Parkstone. The union purchased a plot of land at Longfleet and local man John Tulloch of Parkstone drew up the plans for construction. By 1839 the new building was complete and was situated at the southern end of St Mary's Road. After the workhouse was opened, then Lord of the Manor, Lord de Mauley visited and commented on several points that he considered wrong with the arrangements such as three children to a bed and the water from the water pump being unfit for human consumption. Conditions were often squalid, and going to the workhouse was often a cry of desperation. Families were split up and housed in different wings and the daily regime of workhouse life was gruelling with little rest and little nourishment. Inmates constantly fell ill and many died. It was not until 1903 that an infirmary, designed by local architect H.F.J. Barnes of Poole, was added to the site to treat the ill residents. In 1943 the workhouse was abolished and the buildings became St Mary's Hospital, however by 1979 nearly all of the original buildings were demolished apart from the lodge cottage and the 1903 infirmary. A maternity unit was later built on the site and this is where ghosts of the workhouse years can be seen on some nights. It is said that one father-to-be was leaving the unit when he was approached by a nurse. The first thing he noticed was that the uniform she was wearing was different to midwifes he had just seen. She wore a starched white hat and a grey type of overall like a dress. He had never seen a uniform like it. She was not young although fairly attractive for her age but she had a stern face and his immediate worry was that he had done something wrong and was about to get a telling off. After a while he realised that she was not looking straight at him but behind him as though she was watching something. As he turned round he saw another lady cowering on the ground behind him. He stepped back to allow the nurse to walk towards the lady on the ground and he distinctly heard the nurse call out the name 'Sophia'. He went back into the unit and described what he had seen, including her uniform, but none of the nurses had any idea of what he was talking about. He left the unit confused and was even more astonished when he noticed the two women were gone. It is believed the woman seen crouching down in the grounds (and she has been seen several times) is Sophia Allan. She was resident in the St Mary's Workhouse at the time of the 1881 census and was considered a 'lunatic'. She was sixty-five years old and came from Lytchett. Could the woman in the unusual uniform be the ghost of Jane Gollop? Jane worked at the workhouse at the time Sophia was there and was in charge of all the women who were considered suffering from lunacy, her proper title being female lunatic assistant. She was sixty-six years old when she worked there and so the description the man gave fits. Are these

Artist's impression of the beggar seen at Hunger Hill. (Drawing by Simon Steadman)

Poole Hospital on Longfleet Road where Alfred Russell met his untimely death.

two ladies destined to roam the grounds of the maternity hospital eternally and what, if any, is their unfinished business?

A Wandering Patient?

It seems almost insensitive to report the sighting of a ghost outside Poole General Hospital as sadly hospitals are where many people lose their battle with illnesses each year, however there is only one sighting that is regularly seen and that is the 'wandering patient'.

The hospital stands on Longfleet Road which, as the crow flies, is not far from the town centre. It is a main road and there is rarely a time, day or night, that it is not busy with traffic. The hospital was built after the Second World War during the radical rejuvenation of Poole and was opened by Queen Elizabeth II on 11 July 1969. It was built as a replacement for the old Cornelia Hospital which could not serve the growing town sufficiently.

The sighting reported is that of an old, stooped man wearing an old brown-striped dressing gown, looking down at the pavement at the side entrance to the hospital. Many people have stopped to help him thinking he is an elderly patient who has wandered from the hospital, only to find that when they stop their car he has disappeared. Other reports describe the man as shuffling out into the road but disappearing before he gets to the middle. Due to the sighting's location (being so close to the hospital) it is easy to presume that it must be related to the hospital. On closer investigation it is more likely to be local man Alfred Russell, who in the 1970s lived in a house on Longfleet Road directly opposite the new main hospital site. Mr Russell was suffering from dementia and one night wandered out of his house and went to cross the road. He was dressed in dark nightclothes and a brown dressing gown and sadly a car that just did not see him in the road, hit him. He was killed instantly. Could it be the man seen outside the hospital is just old Alfred trying to get back across the road to his home that he left that fateful night?

Hill with a View

Constitution Hill is located between Poole centre and Parkstone and is approximately one mile north of the town. It is a natural viewpoint at 210ft above sea level, and provides stunning views over the harbour, with Brownsea Island in clear view. Beaches in Poole and the surrounding areas were fenced off with barbed wire during the Second World War as there was the constant threat of invasion. Children had to look for somewhere else to play and Constitution Hill became a popular place for boys to spot the different military boats in the harbour and to watch the Sunderland flying-boats overhead coming in to land. It is still a popular place with locals (and yet somewhat undiscovered by tourists) and provides one of the most beautiful views of the area. Is this why some people choose to return here even after death? On occasions there have been reports of children playing in the area, but these are not normal children. People driving in at night have witnessed the spirits of three or four boys, scruffily dressed, running about on the grassed area of the park. At first the visitors wonder why the young boys are out so late but they are not solid like us; they appear to people in a misty haze as though watched on an old broken or damaged film or from an old projector. They don't appear to enjoy scaring people and although witnesses felt shocked at the sightings, they have also said that felt very happy and carefree watching the boys run and play. One man who saw them said they seemed to be wearing similar clothes to those he wore as a child in the Second World War, so are these wartime boys just returning to play as they did back in the 1940s?

Spiritual Paper Trail

Parkstone Library is located in the centre of Ashley Cross on Britannia Road in a beautiful old building that really stands out from its surroundings. It is here that the spirit of a young man likes to make himself known to the staff who work there. A bell has been heard ringing and several librarians have been subject to whispering in their ears, sudden rises in temperature and noises they can not logically explain. Many of the staff put it to working in an old creaky building but for some seeing was believing. Jim, as one ex-member of staff calls him, is their

Longfleet Road in 1904, long before it became built up.

resident ladies' male ghost who not only likes to tease the women employees but also likes to read the odd book or two. On many mornings staff have apparently found books lying open on particular pages even though they know that no books were left out when they had finished work the day before. One employee decided to follow Jim's paper trail and see if he was leaving them any clues by leaving books open. She started to take note of the page it was left open each time it happened and came up with a chilling message after a couple of months. The message read along the lines of 'fire fire, bell ringing, evacuation, women and children, I could not save them, James'. Having compiled this message the now ex-employee wanted to research into the history of the building. She had not worked there long and knew that the building was old but did not know what it was built for. Her understanding of the message from beyond the grave took on much more importance when she found out from her colleague that it was once the Parkstone Fire Station. Was Jim a fireman? Was he trapped here through his own self-inflicted guilt? The woman felt terrible, as it appeared that maybe Jim could not move on and so one night when she was on her own in the building she decided to leave Jim a message in the same way he had contacted her. She left books out on particular pages that spelt out the message 'James, not your fault, lives were in God's hands, look to the light'. The next morning she returned to the building to open up and noticed all

View of Poole and the harbour from Constitution Hill, early 1900s.

View of Poole and the harbour from Constitution Hill, 2007.

the books were still where she had left them but they were all closed. She felt this was Jim's way of letting her know he had received her message. So has Jim moved on? None of Jim's usual activity is reported anymore though on some occasions staff and members of the public have thought they can feel someone looking over their shoulders or just generally around the building. Hopefully this is James just visiting and not grounded here following the tragedy he could not avoid being involved in.

The Haunted Cow

With the growing trend of trade close to the railway, hotels such as the the Branksome Railway Hotel and the Parkstone Hotel were increasingly popular not only with tourists but also with businessmen. The Parkstone Hotel was situated in Ashley Cross close to main railway line to London and Weymouth. Built in 1855 it is one of the earlier hotels in the suburbs of Poole and it was a thriving hotel in its day. Now the old hotel is home to The Cow Restaurant and multi award-winning freehouse and pub of the year 2007. It's a lively place to go and some believe this is what keeps the spirit of the hotel alive. So many times we see old buildings fall into disrepair but this is as busy now as it ever was. In the 1920s the hotel saw an influx of out-of-the-area visitors, and staff at the hotel worked hard to make their visit pleasant. The area was a growing tourist attraction and happy tourists meant that people would return.

Part of the hotel's past seems to remain in the building today. The ghost of an ex-employee from the 1920s or 1930s is said to reside there still and likes to move items around during the night and also makes themselves known by pushing past people. One example of this was when a waitress was carrying a tray of glasses and was nearly knocked over by a considerable force that pushed past her. She managed to stumble and save the tray of glasses but was shocked by the invisible force that had hit her. Another instance was when the staff had left a bowl of cutlery to be polished the next day. Employees could not believe their luck when they returned the next morning to find that the entire collection of cutlery had been polished and was laid out on a tray. The helpful but strict ghost that seems to haunt this old hotel is thought to be Molly, a waitress and maid who just can't seem to leave the job she obviously loved and wants to see it continue to thrive. Employees of the hotel which has not long been closed, were kept on their toes by this efficacious old employee who likes to make sure tasks are done properly and in the manner she liked them. Staff had the overwhelming feeling they were being watched, as though someone was overseeing what they were doing. The swishing of her long skirt used to alert present-day employees to her presence and guests would feel a sudden rush of icy cold air when they were dining in the restaurant part of the hotel. People would also feel their sheets and bedclothes being tugged if they dared stay in bed too long in the hotel rooms. It seemed Molly was eager to get the rooms and the beds tidied punctually and did not like guests with a lazy disposition. She may be efficacious and like things done to a standard she believes is best but she seems to mean no real harm to anyone and her strictness is only to make sure that the job she did is still being done properly even eighty years after her death.

Coy Pond Murder

On a hot summer's day when you feel like getting away from the hustle and bustle of Poole town centre there is no better place to go than Coy Pond. The area is at the northern end of the English Heritage Grade II Listed gardens which are mainly in Bournemouth, although Poole residents are very proud that 9 acres run into Poole. With weeping willows and alder trees running alongside the stream it is a tranquil area for residents to visit and for local wildlife. The pond was created as a decoy pond in 1888 when the railway embankment was built behind it but little else is known about its history. In 1935 the grounds were leased from Robert Ives of Erpingham, Norfolk and Frederic Ray Eaton of Norwich for 999 years. In 1940 to help with the war effort they were turned into allotments for local produce to be grown for the residents of Branksome. At the end of the war locals wanted to tidy up the area which had become a little overgrown and in 1951 permission was granted for the plots to be turned into pleasure gardens. Since then the area has been managed by the Borough of Poole but has remained largely unchanged.

It is a popular place for people to walk their dogs and several years ago a woman reported meeting a strange boy in a white mackintosh who walked up to her, smiled menacingly then disappeared right in front of her eyes. The woman reported a look of craziness in his eyes, which made her feel ill at ease even though he was only a teenager. It is believed this apparition is that of a local Bournemouth boy who suffered from mental instability and was prone to acts of very strange behaviour. One day he decided to walk the two miles through the gardens starting near the pier in Bournemouth wearing just his white mackintosh, until he reached Coy Pond. He had been acting very strangely that day and in a fit of unexplained rage approached a man in his garden near the pond and hacked him to death with the scythe the man was using to cut his grass. He left the body of the man where he was and as though nothing had happened walked the two miles home in his blood-stained raincoat. At home he hid the coat in his room where his mother found it two days later and contacted the police. The boy was tried and was sentenced to three years imprisonment. The courts were lenient because of his mental state, however he passed away just two years after his release. Is this the little boy in the white mackintosh the woman saw returning to the scene of his crime?

On the Beat

Many people do not believe in ghosts or anything of a paranormal nature but some things are too strange to describe as anything else. Ringwood Road is a busy part of Poole, running through the suburb of Parkstone, and it was on this road that a local couple in 1998 literally had to rub their eyes with disbelief.

The man had just picked up his wife from her place of work and it was 11.45 p.m. on a fairly dark November night but the road was well lit with street lights. Travelling towards them on the other side of the road was a dark figure on a bicycle and the couple commented to each other how stupid it was for someone to be out this late at night on a bicycle with no lights. As it got closer they realised the man was wearing a policeman's uniform and helmet but not of the present day. It looked as though it was from the turn of the century. By then they could also see the very old-fashioned bicycle he was riding, nothing like you would be able to buy in the 1990s. Both commented that it looked as though it should be in a museum. Just at that moment, as they watched in amazement, a white van came up behind the policeman on his bike and then passed right through him, overtaking the couple's car at the same time. They were obviously worried that they had just witnessed a hit-and-run, stopped their car and got out, but the road was quiet. They could see the van in the distance but there was no policeman and no bicycle anywhere to be seen.

The Pottery Man and his Ghostly Smoke

Branksome is a suburb of Poole, which borders Parkstone, Branksome Park and Westbourne (a suburb of Bournemouth). Up until the late nineteenth century most of this area was undeveloped heath. It was not until the arrival of the railway station and a few houses that Branksome became a popular place to live, being undeveloped and in close proximity to Poole town and Bournemouth. Today it is largely residential but if you look closely you can see clues to its Victorian and Edwardian past. The shopping area that houses DIY and home-furnishing stores, was, until the mid-twentieth century, Poole Clay and Pottery Works which would have employed many of the local Branksome and Parkstone residents. Some of the old, grey outbuildings still remain and it is around these that the figure of a man has been seen.

A manager of one of the large stores was closing up his shop one night and his wife was waiting for him in the car. She was observing a short, old man dressed in grey and wearing an old-style cloth cap. He appeared to be shovelling something in the road. She believed that she watched him for a good five minutes until her attention was attracted by her husband knocking on the car window to be let in. She joked about the man but when they looked back he had gone. She pointed out where the man had been and what he had appeared to have been doing. They drove closer to the outbuildings and saw wisps of grey smoke rising from one of the outbuildings. Knowing the premises were empty and disused, and fearing a tramp or children had ventured inside and started a fire, the woman screeched the car to a halt to let her husband get out and have a look. He could hear a clanging of metal striking metal but could not pinpoint where it was coming from. As he got nearer to the old buildings, the smoke stopped and the site fell suddenly silent. A little spooked by the sudden silence of the site he got back in the car and they left. Could they have encountered one of the ghostly workmen from the old pottery and clay works that are said to haunt this area?

The Romantic Couple

In the heart of Parkstone and Branksome is Branksome Recreation Ground. A beautiful park, it offers all-round use to local junior and senior amateur football clubs, the circus when it comes to town and of course a walking ground for the hundreds of dog owners in the heavily populated residential area surrounding it. In the 1970s it was the centre of local media attraction when residents made reports to the police of UFO sightings when large orange and yellow flashing lights appeared over the park. It is also the home to a rather amorous but scarily faceless couple that many people have seen, oddly since the UFO sightings. One of the local residents that had seen this odd pair told me that she had been walking her two dogs in the park one evening and she could not help noticing the couple sitting on the bank in front of the trees canoodling romantically. She was walking her dogs, as usual around the perimeter of the park (before a pathway was made) and the couple actually made her jump, as she had not seen them as she was walking along and it was getting quite dark. They were on her left and as she passed them she felt an odd sense of unease which she had not felt before even though she had walked her dog hundreds of times in that particular area. A rustle in the trees behind them made her swing around and shine her torch in their general direction. She thought she may have startled them with the torch and so called out an apology. The couple stopped their romantic liaison and turned to face her but to her amazement she could not make out any facial features. She could see the lady had long hair and the man had short hair but because of the failing light could not make out what they were wearing. One thing she was sure about was their lack of faces. She could feel her heart beating loudly in her chest, stammered another 'sorry' in their direction and continued walking. When she was about 20ft away, she turned round, still not able to believe what she had seen and the couple had gone. The incredible thing is that if they were there and had left when they were disturbed, they would have had to pass near her to get out of the park or they would still have been seen walking away. Neither were the case and the shaking woman cut short her walk and made her way home.

Demon Dog on the Heath

Canford Heath is one of the only remaining patches of lowland heath in the county. It is hard to imagine but hundreds of years ago most of Dorset would have had this type of landscape. This part of the Poole district retains an enchanting sense of wilderness and is listed as a Site of Special Scientific Interest. In 2005 a woman and her elderly mother were crossing the heath while on an afternoon stroll. The two women were shocked when they suddenly heard a growling noise coming from the nearby heather. As they approached, they could see the eyes of a creature and described them as 'burning red in colour and glowing'. When they got really close to investigate they were surprised by a louder growl, described almost like a roar. The couple then fled the area as fast as they could but could hear the sound of something running behind them. Exhausted, they stopped when they reached a road and were relieved to find nothing was behind them. Not wanting to stay around they decided to make their way home. This is not the only tale of a demonic creature on the heath. One man told me that in the 1930s his father used to tell him that if he stayed on the heath after dark the 'demon dog' would hunt him down. Scared that this was true, he and his friends would never wander the heath at night. Was this just a canny way of controlling children's movements or was the legend of the demon dog true? We may never know for sure but you will be hard pushed to find a local that will spend a night alone on the heath. Would you?

Private Hauntings in Poole

Your home is supposed to be your castle and sanctuary but some local families got more than they bargained for when they bought their homes. The following information is from the actual people involved and some of their names have been changed to protect their identities. Thank you all so much for coming forward to tell your experiences.

Mystery Man

The family first noticed strange goings-on in the 1980s when objects would disappear from their house. This was always put down to their mislaying things but soon they noticed that the items that went missing were always from the kitchen table. These were just everyday objects that you would find in most houses.

Jane, a resident of the house, swore that on many occasions she had seen the figure of a man walk from one end of her kitchen to the other and into a corner where he simply disappeared as if walking through the wall. He was dressed in black and had dark hair, but she only ever saw a rear view of him, and it was always a 'corner of the eye' sighting so she was never able to get a good look at him.

Another occurrence was when Jane and Colleen (another female resident in the house) were in their respective bedrooms getting ready for bed and settling down for the night when they both reported hearing the sound of someone downstairs in their kitchen. Not only could they clearly hear someone in the house but it also sounded as though they were at the sink washing up as they could clearly hear the clatter of dishes and splashing of water. This alarmed the women as they knew that were alone in the house apart from their very young children who were sleeping in adjacent rooms. The women were too worried to enter the kitchen to investigate as they would have had to go downstairs and the middle of the stairs was a place they always, for no apparent reason, felt ill at ease. That night was no exception.

These occurrences were now starting to worry the women and the final straw came when Jane witnessed the full apparition of a man in the kitchen. This time she was able to view him directly and watched as he walked from one side of the room to the other, and as usual disappeared through the wall. Jane could not help but scream, and ran immediately into the lounge and told Colleen what she had seen. In a state of understandable panic the women, not wanting to exit the house through the kitchen or adjoining hallway, gathered up the children and all climbed out of the lounge windows. They all ran the half-a-mile to the house of Colleen's mother, Rose, refusing to return to the property. They never lived in the house in Melbury Avenue again.

Jane moved in with a friend and Colleen continued living with Rose. Rose had a work acquaintance that knew of a psychic and paranormal investigator named Benson Herbert (this is his real name). They contacted him on behalf of the family and he agreed to visit the property with a team of his colleagues to see if there was anything they could pick up on. They arranged to meet outside the house but Jane could not bring herself to be there and gave permission for Matt, a young friend of Colleen's brother, to enter on her behalf through the lounge window so he was able to let the others in.

Mr Herbert believed the house to be on a leyline and could immediately sense great sadness within the house. Unverified rumours abounded that someone had hung themselves in the house, although this was not disclosed to him. He did, however, also predict rather strangely that there would be a suicide connected to the group in the near future. This shocked everyone there as it was not something they were expecting to hear, but they put it to the back of their minds and continued through the house with him. Sensing a lot of spirit activity the team and

Mr Herbert cleansed and blessed the house and since then no more activity has been reported though the family no longer live in the building.

Some time later Mr Herbert's chilling prediction was to come true when Matt, the first person to enter the house after it had been abandoned, took his own life. Matt was homeless and as he was a friend of the family Rose gave him somewhere to sleep and opened up her home to him. He never got on with his own mother and looked up to Colleen's mother as his own. He was always a happy and carefree young man and the family report that he always seemed to be smiling. A few months after the investigation at the property Matt died of a self-inflicted drug overdose. When he lived at Rose's house it was always joked that he would come in at night and cook a fried onion sandwich, and for months after his death at around the same time every evening Rose and the family could smell onions frying. It was a tragic loss of a young life but was this his way of making himself known to the family that had done so much for him?

Jane was so traumatised by the events that she spent time in a local psychiatric hospital and later turned to religion as a way of dealing with what she had been through. To this day the events still haunt her and she does not talk about them. Benson Herbert the psychical researcher who was also the director of the Paraphysical Laboratory in London, set up his own laboratory in Wiltshire specialising in physical phenomena. Later in his career he travelled around the world which included a visit to Russia where he worked extensively with psychic Nina Kulagina. Benson Herbert, a master of his work, sadly passed away in 1991 aged seventy-nine.

Not my Jean!

The second tale of a private haunting in Poole is not so tragic and was told to me by John and Shirley Hatton of Canford Heath. They have lived in their house for twenty-three years and even though they have considered moving many times they are never quite sure that little Jean will come with them. Little Jean is the spirit of a cat that lives in their house and has been seen by many of their friends, family and callers to the house in general. Very rightly, if they do move they are worried that unlike a living cat, they will not be able to catch Jean and take her with them so they prefer to stay put.

When Jean was alive she was not their cat but the pet of the lady that owned the house before them. The couple don't even know her name nor did their elderly neighbour although she knew the previous owner and that she had a cat. The name Jean was given to the spirit of the cat by John and Shirley as the animal seemed to like ripping up John's best denim jeans. This is how the story of Jean starts.

It was the middle of summer and the couple retired to bed leaving the window open for fresh air. At about 2 a.m. John woke to the sound of a cat howling and try as he might he could not sleep through it. Although the pair did not have any pets of their own, other residents owned cats and he often heard them howling to each other at night. On this occasion he thought the noise was coming from within the house and so decided to investigate, thinking that maybe one had got trapped in garage that adjoined their house. After checking the garage and the rest of the house the noise stopped and John decided to go back to bed. He was woken less than an hour later by the sound of a cat meowing in the room. He jumped out of bed but could not see anything. Getting slightly annoyed now as he had to be up early the next morning, he decided to shut the windows, and in his frustration did so with quite a bang. As he did he heard a scurrying sound as if something had been scared out of the room. A little perplexed he went back to bed and managed to sleep the rest of the night undisturbed. By the next, almost forgetting about the events of the previous night, he ate his breakfast as normal, said goodbye to Shirley and set off for a day's work. Shirley was not working that day and set about the housework. She decided to do some washing which she went to collect from the bedroom. John's jeans were in the corner of the bathroom where the basket was overflowing, and to Shirley's amazement his brand pair had several long claw-like scratches in them. She did not see much point in washing them and left them out to remind herself to ask John what had happened to them. When he returned and saw the jeans he was as confused as his wife, having left them the night before in one piece. From this point on the newly named 'Jean' made herself known in several ways.

When sitting in front of the television it was a regular occurrence for one of the pair to feel a sensation as though a cat was jumping onto their laps. Guests to the house with animal allergies would start sneezing and coughing, but the first sighting of Jean was when a friend of Shirley's came round with her dog. The Border collie had to be put back in the car as it would not stop barking in a corner of the room and was trying to get at something that he could obviously see! A couple of days later another friend called in and when he came back from the bathroom appeared to stop and talk to himself. Shirley could not understand it until he asked Shirley when they had acquired a cat. He described the cat and the couple went next door and spoke to the elderly owner. He remembered the cat that had lived in the house and was able to describe her in exactly the same way as the friend had – a small, short-haired ginger tabby with a white-tipped tail. To this day 'Jean' still appears to people, knocks over things in the house, teases local dogs and demands attention in general just like any cat does. However, John is now very careful about where he hangs his trousers!

Victorian Lady

The final private haunting story comes from a couple that live in a modest terraced house behind Poole Stadium. Built in the 1930s, their house is one of the oldest in Poole but as we hear so often, haunted properties do not have to be ancient. They live alone in the house but have many visitors. One of those visitors appears to enjoy hanging around a little longer than the rest. The couple, who have lived in the house for two years, have always felt there was someone else there with them. They would hear odd noises, unexplained smells, feel cold spots even on the hottest summer afternoons and would put items in one room only to find they turned up minutes later elsewhere. While they are sometimes a little spooked by the goings-on, open-minded in their views, they are not scared by the presence. They have only seen their visitor twice but enough to know she means them no harm. The lady of the house has seen their guest at the tops of their stairs smiling down at her. The ghost is tall and slim, dressed in a beautiful grey, taffeta dress and long black buttoned-up coat. She has long auburn hair, tied up on her head and looks happy. Her attire is very Victorian and in fact the land the houses (and indeed Poole Stadium) are built on is the site of a Victorian landfill and so you can only imagine the period energy that may be in that area. The couple is not in any way perturbed by this and is quite happy to be sharing their home with this lovely spectral lady!

Other local titles published by The History Press

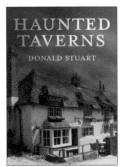

Haunted Taverns

DONALD STUART

From heart-stopping accounts of apparitions, manifestations and related supernatural phenomena to first-hand encounters with ghouls and spirits, this collection of stories takes the reader on a chilling tour of haunted inns all over England. From hair-raising tales about a fourteenth-century pub with its own ghost duck, the phantom who leaves a strong smell of rum and tobacco throughout an ancient inn, the beer jug that fills itself up in the middle of the night to a Devil's dog the size of a calf that disappears into the walls of the old inn it haunts, this book will bring goose-bumps to those who dare open its cover.

978 07524 4347 8

Haunted Cardiff and the Valleys

SOUTH WALES PARANORMAL RESEARCH

Journey through the darker side of Cardiff and the surrounding valleys, an area steeped in ancient history and ghostly goings-on. Because of its rich cultural past, it is riddled with numerous tales of ghosts and hauntings, both old and new. Drawing on extensive research and interviews with first-hand witnesses, South Wales Paranormal Research have put together this chilling collection of sightings and mysterious happenings, mostly from the last ten years. Featuring ghostly cars and ships, mysterious policemen and figures in country lanes, this book will appeal to anyone interested in the paranormal or those who wish to read more about tales and legends from Cardiff's shadowy past.

978 07524 4378 2

Haunted London

JAMES CLARK

This collection of stories contains new and well-known spooky tales from famous sights and buildings in the centre of London. Drawing on historical and contemporary sources *Haunted London* contains a chilling range of ghostly phenomena. From the monk ghost who clanks his chains on Buckingham Palace's terrace every Christmas Day, the phantom horse-bus that occasionally rattles along Bayswater Road to the haunted Pig Tree, a terrifying apparition that frequents Green Park, the colourful tales featured here create a scary selection of ghostly goings-on that is bound to captivate anyone interested in the supernatural history of the area.

978 07524 4459 8

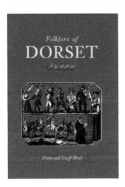

Folklore of Dorset

FRAN AND GEOFF DOEL

Folklore of Dorset explores the rich heritage of the county's traditions, seasonal customs and songs. Included are saints' lore and smugglers, wife sales, wrecking, witchcraft, wise men and West Gallery Music, hill figures, hempseed divination and holy wells, mummers' plays, May garlands and Maypoles, Oosers and Oak Apple Day, bonfires and Beating the Bounds. The sources used include the poems and non-fiction of William Barnes, Thomas Hardy, the historian of Dorset John Hutchins, the Victorian and early twentieth-century folklorist John Udal and the Hammond Brothers' collection of Dorset folksongs. Nearly 100 fascinating photographs illustrate the text and there is an appendix of a full mummers' play.

978 07524 3989 1

If you are interested in purchasing other books published by The History Press, or in case you have difficulty finding any of our books in your local bookshop, you can also place orders directly through our website
www.thehistorypress.co.uk